what
to
eat

what
to
eat

The Ten Things You Really Need to Know to Eat Well and Be Healthy!

LUISE LIGHT, M.S., ED.D.

McGraw·Hill

New York   Chicago   San Francisco   Lisbon   London   Madrid   Mexico City
Milan   New Delhi   San Juan   Seoul   Singapore   Sydney   Toronto

The McGraw·Hill Companies

Library of Congress Cataloging-in-Publication Data

Light, Luise.
    What to eat : the ten things you really need to know to eat well and be healthy! /
Luise Light.
        p.   cm.
    Includes index.
    ISBN 0-07-145313-X
    1. Nutrition.   2. Health.   3. Weight loss.   I. Title.

RA784.L546   2006
613.2'5—dc22   2005027374

1 2 3 4 5 6 7 8 9 0   FGR/FGR   0 9 8 7 6 5

ISBN 0-07-145313-X

McGraw-Hill books are available at special quantity discounts to use as premiums and sales promotions, or for use in corporate training programs. For more information, please write to the Director of Special Sales, Professional Publishing, McGraw-Hill, Two Penn Plaza, New York, NY 10121-2298. Or contact your local bookstore.

What to Eat: The Ten Things You Really Need to Know to Eat Well and Be Healthy! is intended solely for informational and educational purposes and not as personal medical advice. Please consult your health-care professional if you have any questions about your health. Stories and personal histories related to weight, nutrition, and health in this book have been changed to protect the identity of individuals who provided them. Neither the author nor the publisher has received financial support from the food industry or groups that represent its special interests.

This book is printed on acid-free paper.

I dedicate this book with love and gratitude to the women healers and teachers whose advice and perspectives created in me a passion for the truth and a dedication to sharing what I've learned with others who are willing to consider how these words may benefit them:

My daughters, Sara Light-Waller and Orrea Light

Professor Orrea Pye, Ph.D.

Meredith Young-Sowers, D.D.

Gladys Taylor McGarey, M.D., M.D.(H)

Patricia Kaminski

Juliette de Bairacli Levy

Mary Sparrowdancer

Linda Haltinner, Chiropractic Physician

Carolyn Dean, M.D., N.D.

Annemarie F. Crocetti, Dr.P.H.

And in loving memory, Annie Toglia

CONTENTS

ACKNOWLEDGMENTS

Behind a book are the many individuals who are instrumental and especially helpful in bringing it into the world.

Heartfelt thanks go to my editor, Judith McCarthy, whose clear vision, steady support, unshakeable faith, and wise suggestions were critical to making this book emerge. I am grateful for the opportunity to work with her, and I hope this is the beginning of a long, mutually beneficial relationship.

It was my great good fortune to be "found" by an extraordinary agent, Jacques de Spoelberch, whose publishing savvy is only exceeded by his grace, humor, and wisdom. Thank you, Jacques, for believing in me and the book and finding us a good home.

To Meredith Young-Sowers, D.D., whose encouragement and belief in my life purpose brought me back to the work I left but that never left me.

Gratitude to my daughters, Sara and Orrea, who kept telling me it was time to write "the book." I finally took their advice. I am blessed by their encouragement and eagerness to help with tasks both big and small over many years.

Special thanks to Fran Kemmer, Ronney Aden, Phyllis Herman, Jane Smolnik, Suzan Sutton for advice, suggestions, and encouragement in the early stages of the book's development.

Thanks to my friends and colleagues who acted as readers and provided timely comments, studies, phone numbers, and perspectives that enriched the book: Mary Sparrowdancer, Pam Killeen, Dr. Shanthy Bowman, Paul Geffert, Cathy White.

And to all the others, too numerous to mention, who shared their experiences, tried out strategies from the book, and taught me what it takes to commit to change, my deep gratitude will always be yours.

INTRODUCTION

You picked up this book because you have questions about how to eat well. Eating has become confusing. One week you hear that eating too much meat increases your risk of getting colon cancer. The next week you hear just the opposite. One week milk helps you lose weight; the next week this claim is considered bogus. One news story says breast cancer has nothing to do with how much fat you eat, the next one says it does. Should we be eating low-fat or low-carb? Are the new USDA guidelines (my pyramid.gov) the best ones to follow, or should we just forget them and buy what's convenient?

There's so much conflicting information about nutrition and health. If you're like most Americans, you believe there are good and bad foods and that eating too much fat is bad, but you haven't a clue how to eat less. You watch your portion sizes but don't know if you are eating too many or just the right amount of calories.

Confusion has grown beyond all reasonable limits. Despite a deluge of "healthy products" and daily bombardments of health claims in the media, more people are overweight than ever before. That's why you need this book, *What to Eat*, because it offers the answers you're looking for.

When I left Washington in 1995, I was convinced that I had left the field of nutrition for good. I was disappointed and depressed that good nutrition and healthy eating, subjects fundamental to "life, liberty, and the pursuit of happiness," were obscured by lobbyists and their allies in government. A seemingly impenetrable wall of distortion had been erected to block new thinking that could interfere with the way food was made, promoted, or sold.

After fourteen years working as a nutritionist in two government agencies, I went to work as the director of the Institute for Science in Society (ISIS), a small non-profit think tank. The last ISIS white paper we released to the press was on infectious problems in the U.S. meat supply. The ISIS report documented the poor sanitary practices and the government's archaic and negligent inspection procedures that were directly to blame for these outbreaks.

We were just beginning to hear about the British epidemic of mad cow disease, but we were reassured by USDA officials that the problem was localized to Britain and couldn't happen in North America. However, my colleagues at the National Institutes of Health, who were infectious disease specialists, already knew that mad cow disease grew out of changes in how animal feeds were manufactured and that our cows were being fed the same way. They assured me that unless we started making changes in our feeding and inspection practices, the problem could be just as deadly here.

Industry reaction to the ISIS report was furious, and then, as the press lost interest, it turned deadly quiet. I left Washington and moved to Connecticut to a job as health editor of *Vegetarian Times* magazine. I wasn't a vegetarian, but the ISIS meat report gave me enough credibility to be hired by a magazine that celebrated meatless lifestyles. I ended up as the editorial director of a small New England book publisher and training institute, as well as a freelance writer/editor. But I continued to follow news of nutrition and to read reports that described the horrific, escalating rates of obesity, diabetes, and other diet-related diseases engulfing North Americans of all ages and much of the world as well.

I kept puzzling about it, asking myself, what's going on? What was it about our food, lifestyles, and environment that was plunging us into such a devastating abyss? What could we do as individuals to avoid becoming victims of these terrible plagues? Was there a way of eating and living that would save us? Little by little, I was drawn back into the field of nutrition, determined to use my skills to investigate the problem and find solutions to offer people.

In the past twenty years, the time frame in which obesity and chronic diseases have hit us so hard, we have experienced major changes in how we eat, what we eat, and the nutritional content of our foods and diets. If there were answers to our problems, they had to come from those areas.

One profound change was globalization, and most of the changes in our foods were made to enable us to deliver similar foods and drinks to consumers in Malaysia, Madagascar, Ecuador, and Nigeria as well as North America. The innovative foods we began to eat were designed for long shelf lives and a wide variety of climates. But our Paleolithic bodies don't handle innovative factory foods very well, and we are paying a high price for these quick and easy foods.

This is a book for people concerned about what to eat to stay healthy, lose weight, and to the extent possible, avoid common chronic diseases. There are so many different approaches to healthy eating that it's hard to know which approach will work best for you. *What to Eat* is not a primer to prove that any single philosophy of eating is more correct than others. What is offered is a tour through the changing landscape of our nutritional problems and clear answers to your questions about how to eat well and be healthy even as the world of food changes around us.

In addition to offering a road map for healthy eating, this guide helps expose the underbelly of our national obsession with food; reveals facts about ingredients in popular foods that could adversely affect our health and weight; provides insights into how food is marketed to make us buy it; and shows how starved we are for reliable information.

But even more fundamental than these issues is the sense of disempowerment many of us experience when dealing with food. It's as if we are strangers in an alien food landscape. Two-thirds of Americans make food decisions based on what we hear, see, and read in the media, but the media only tell us the food and nutrition stories that are endorsed by corporate sponsors. If you never look at food through another lens, it is easy to assume those are the only facts worth knowing.

Yet most of us have an innate ability to recognize that food is more than something that quiets our internal signals of distress when we're hungry. Food is the raw material that the alchemy of our bodies transmutes into sinew, muscle, and gland and into the raw resources for the millions of chemical reactions governing how our bodies, minds, and emotions function as we grow from infancy to childhood to adolescence to maturity.

What to Eat is written for both men and women because diet-related health risks affect men and women equally. Biologically, we are far more similar than we are different, a conclusion supported by the striking parallels in men's and women's rates of chronic disease.

The conclusion to this particular story is this: we need to take back the reins regarding what and how to eat on a personal level, in our families, and for the environment. For too long we have allowed others, with different agendas than ours, to make these decisions for us. As you will see when you read this book, we can't afford to do that any longer. You must decide for yourself what is good and healthful for you to eat. All the experts in the world don't know as much as you do about that.

what
to
eat

1

Eating Shapes Your Fate

Things are seldom what they seem, skim milk masquerades as cream.

—W. S. GILBERT

When Alan W. called me in the middle of the day, I suspected he was in some kind of crisis. Alan had asked me to help him lose weight. When I met him, he was seventy pounds overweight, and he had already lost one hundred pounds on the Atkins diet. Alan was frustrated because his weight loss had stalled, so together we laid out an exercise and low-carbohydrate, moderate-calorie plan. Everything seemed to be going fine until he called and told me that something weird had happened to him.

That morning, at the monthly team meeting, Alan's boss had passed around bagels and cream cheese. Alan couldn't resist and polished off one and a half of the hefty bagels. In a short time, he felt "wiped—as if someone disabled me with a Taser gun." He had left a call for his physician, but he was feeling better now and wondered whether I could help him figure out, "What's going on?"

I agreed that it was a good idea to speak with his physician and suggested that he might have experienced a massive insulin response to all the sugar that was released into his bloodstream from the bagels. "But I'm not diabetic," he protested. Possibly prediabetic, I suggested, urging him to check it out and explaining what I thought had happened to his metabolism.

Eating a large amount of breads and rolls made with refined white flour, or crackers, cookies, pies, cakes, and other sweets, can increase your risk of type 2 diabetes. This most common type of diabetes is now an epidemic among obese adults in the United States. I told Alan that eating the bagels could have created a spike in his blood sugar and prompted his pancreas to release a large surge of insulin to clear the excess sugar from his bloodstream. This flood of insulin then lowered his blood sugar below where it had started. This type of sugar roller coaster, repeated many times, eventually can exhaust the pancreas' ability to produce insulin, resulting in diabetes. When I explained this to Alan, I underscored the importance of eating moderate amounts of vegetables, fruits, and whole grains, which were his best carbohydrate choices. This, along with the low-carbohydrate moderate-calorie weight loss plan we had discussed, would help him lose weight and minimize his risk of diabetes and other health problems.

The way you eat, Alan had just learned in a visceral way, controls your destiny. Alan, like most of the people in my weight loss and nutrition classes, was underinformed about nutrition and didn't really understand that how you eat directly affects your survival and the likelihood of developing major degenerative diseases. Most of my students had seen the USDA's food pyramid, but it had made no lasting impression on them because they didn't perceive it as a lifeline against disease.

With two-thirds of American adults now overweight or obese, plainly something has gone very wrong in the United States. The government has been advising people what to eat for one hundred years, but over the last twenty, either the message stopped getting through or an obesity virus has ravaged the country. Why were intelligent people like my students caught in the grip of a silent killer, obesity, that made the government's nutrition advice seem irrelevant?

The Good Ship Nutrition

Many experts offer advice about nutrition, but few clearly and comprehensively tell you what eating lifestyles are the healthiest based on what we know today. Which approaches are most likely to help you keep your weight in check and your body in balance—as safe as possible from hazards in the environment and in our foods?

While it's not possible to live 100 percent risk-free, this book explains how to tip the balance in your favor. It offers Ten Rules for Healthy Eating, a new simpler food pyramid guide, and a step-by-step eating plan that breaks through the nutrition confusion, helps you filter out the disinformation that abounds, shows how to protect your kids from ad-pollution, and arms you with strategies that will help you confidently make smart, sane, safe, and enjoyable food choices. Yes, food is supposed to be a pleasure, not a prescription like medicine! This is not a case of the nutrition police trying to confiscate your Twinkies and hamburgers. It is a matter of giving you tools to choose foods you relish in the amounts and forms best suited for your health and well-being.

This is a time of enormous technological change; some have called it the third industrial revolution. Food is a big part of this revolution—how it's grown and manufactured, what's in it, where it comes from, and how well it meets our nutrition and health needs. These issues require reexamination because so many of our traditional approaches to food and nourishment are no longer valid. Most of us are only dimly aware of the changes food has undergone in recent years even though these changes can—and probably do—affect us profoundly.

Some of the affects of these changes can be seen in the rising rates of obesity and chronic disease in our country. We have come to accept the idea that our lives probably will be shortened by one of these disasters; however, a health catastrophe doesn't have to be your fate.

Think of it this way. Each of us has a personal nutrition account—our bodies—in which we invest important resources for the future. If we make the daily, weekly, and monthly deposits designed to keep our minds, bodies, and spirits strong and resilient, we can prevent, delay, or mitigate most of the dire health conditions we fear. It certainly seems worth it, but so many of us find making lifestyle changes so much more difficult than it should be. The big reason behind this difficulty is that we're continuously massaged by subtle, misleading persuasions to forget the consequences and indulge today. We have been trained to think that we can "have it all" and that it's "cool" to dine at life's great smorgasbord believing that there will be no consequences.

A few legislators, alarmed by the intensifying attempts of the junk food lobby to mislead the public, have proposed regulations restricting the sale of junk foods or levying "fat taxes" on high-fat foods sold to kids. They recognize that it's tough to instill good food habits when kids are subjected to daily barrages of candy, soft drink, and fast-food ads during the hours they watch TV. How do you ask your kids to battle the bulge when the ads constantly tell them that "fun foods" will make them happy, popular, and successful?

What to Eat doesn't pull any punches. It lays out how we are failing to curb the obesity crisis and why our government promotes grocery manufacturers, supermarket chains, convenience stores, and fast-food outlets over the public's health. Once you are armed with the facts and the tools, you will be able to chart your own nutrition course by investing your food dollars where they will do you the most good.

If you are like the students in my nutrition and weight loss classes, you probably have a lot of questions about nutrition, including:

- Does it make sense to pay the extra dollars to buy organic or are the differences too small to be worthwhile?

- Is tap water as good for you as bottled water?
- Does eating lots of vegetables lower your cancer risk?
- How can I boost my immunity so I don't get sick so often?
- Is there anything I can do to have more energy and feel less sleepy and tired all the time?
- Do I need extra vitamins?
- Why can't I lose weight when I eat so little?
- Is a low-fat or low-carbohydrate diet better for you in the long run?
- Are soy products safe?
- What are good fats?
- What sweeteners are best to use?
- Can I still have my favorite treat foods once in a while?"

What strikes me about these questions is that people are looking for answers and they can't find them. There is so much conflicting information available that they don't know what or whom to believe. In the past, most people believed the government had the final word on nutrition. But now, many people don't trust the government to tell them the truth. They've read or heard too much about how the government lines itself up with the food industry. They don't know how, but they are aware of subtle media manipulations to keep them buying and eating more.

Despite a superabundance of information on the Internet and reams of nutrition and diet books in bookstores, my students tell me they feel like nutrition "patsies," told something is *bad* one day and that it's *good* the next. The good news is that while we don't have all the answers, we know enough to buy and eat healthier. Nutrition is not that obscure. The problem is that it's in the interest of certain groups whose business is to sell food to blur the lines between what's good and bad. The less we know, the easier it is to sell us a bill of goods about what to eat. But you don't have to buy into these con jobs.

Most of us consume about sixteen foods and beverages daily, excluding water. That means we have sixteen opportunities each day to consume the thousands of nutritional elements—vitamins, minerals, trace elements, amino acids, carbohydrates, fats, and antioxidants—our bodies need to function at their peak: mentally, physically, and emotionally.

Despite all the knowledge that's been amassed by research laboratories over the globe, two-thirds of Americans eat a diet rated as poor by the government, falling short of recommended levels of many essential nutrients. Add to that the large numbers of people who overconsume fat, sugar, salt, and calories, and we are left with a small part of the public who are well-nourished—less than 10 percent of us, according to the USDA. How can it be that the people in the richest, strongest, and most dominant country in the world—as well as the world's breadbasket—are so sadly lacking in nutrition?

Getting the nutrition you need requires planning. There is no single food or formula that can deliver all the nutrition your body requires. Even though we want to eat right, the way we live today—frantically hurtling from one activity to the next and multitasking through our daily to-do lists—there's no time for planning and checking out facts. Instead, we rely on what's old and familiar, the brands we know and the media experts we are used to going to for advice, although their first priority may be marketing to us rather than objectively informing us.

Have you ever wondered if the food packages on the shelves and in the freezers of your supermarket contain foods like those you enjoyed in your mother and grandmother's kitchens? Macaroni and cheese, we assume, is macaroni and cheese, despite the lengthy list of chemical-named ingredients on the side of the box, ingredients that never saw the light of day in Grandma's kitchen.

Experts in government and academia assure us that these chemical concoctions are the nutritional equivalents of the traditional foods they mimic, but they don't taste exactly the same or satisfy us in the way the originals did. We have a vague sense that things made in a laboratory can't be as good for us as those made from scratch in our kitchen. But what can we do? Most of the time we lay aside our concerns because we barely have time to get supper on the table, much less make it from scratch. Pressured for time, we make do with a casserole-in-a-box, a ready-to-eat frozen meal, or takeout, the basic three food groups most Americans bank on for supper.

We have made the global food industry our national nutrition nanny. But is that wise? The big corporations' priority is getting the biggest profit from every dollar they invest in food, even if that means shortchanging us nutritionally. Why else would $400 million be spent annually on advertising sugared breakfast cereals, cookies, and sugary drinks, among other kid foods?

Why else would artery-clogging trans-fatty acids—known to be toxic to our hearts—still be a common ingredient in frozen dinners and desserts, french fries, breads, cookies, and crackers? And why else would some of the most popular commercial brands of canned soups contain as much salt per serving as the National Academy of Sciences recommends for an entire day? Commercial, highly processed foods, associated with the overconsumption of fat, saturated fat, trans-fats, sugars, sweeteners, white flour, and artificial additives are culprits in our national nutrition decline and characteristic of poor quality diets associated with diabetes, heart disease, and common cancers.

The track record of the food industry in responding to our national nutrition crisis has been slow, erratic, and lethargic. Reassuring public relations campaigns and food ads are the industry's first reaction, followed by reformulating products minimally to deflect negative backlash and speculation that certain foods are contributing to obesity. Yes, manufacturers can add a few grams of whole grain to children's breakfast cereals, but that doesn't change them from breakfast candy, with almost half their calories from sugars, to health foods.

The Western diet is an experiment waiting to be analyzed. We are eating foods and ingredients unknown to our ancestors and even to our parents and grandparents. Our foods have changed dramatically, but our nutritional requirements still mirror those of our ancient Paleolithic ancestors. We have no direct, hard data as to whether the innovative techno foods and eating practices of the twenty-first century meet our evolutionary nutritional needs, but there are disquieting signs that they do not.

Changes in our laws as well as our lifestyles have created problems of pollution in the air, water, and soil, as well as in our food. Toxic levels of mercury and arsenic contaminate our streams and rivers, cancer-causing asbestos and industrial emissions pollute our air, and deadly pesticides used in growing our food collect in the soil and in our bodies. Anything that filters through the environment infiltrates our bodies. Pollutants stored in our tissues cause damage to our immune and neuroendocrine systems, impairing our health and inhibiting our ability to digest, absorb, and utilize the nutrients we consume.

Over the past twenty years, the time in which the changes in our foods have been the most dramatic, the number of people with severe gastrointestinal problems has increased fourfold, suggesting that allergies or intolerances to some food ingredients in widespread use may be fueling these inflammatory reactions.

Pollution can raise nutrient requirements leading to nutritional shortfalls that interfere with growth, reproduction, bone strength, muscle tone, and body functions. When our digestive systems are overburdened by pollution, our bodies work overtime to compensate, eventually exhausting the body's ability to respond and triggering biochemical imbalances that can lead to chronic health problems.

The syndrome of nutritional malaise, characterized by too many calories and overweight coupled with multiple nutrient shortfalls, food sensitivities, and gastrointestinal (GI) disorders and inflammation is quite common today. As many as 70 million adults suffer from some form of digestive malady, more than those with diabetes, heart disease, or cancer. Obesity in itself creates a chronic inflammatory condition in which overactive fat cells signal the body to produce more inflammation messengers and less anti-inflammation hormones.

Along with GI distress, more people are experiencing symptoms of mental and physical decline including memory loss, loss of balance, depression, "road rage," low energy, "mind-freeze," eye strain, generalized aches and pains, abdominal discomfort, headaches, and frequent colds and flu. These classic signs of biochemical chaos, unless corrected, can develop into full-blown heart disease, diabetes, high blood pressure, cancers, osteoporosis, asthma, arthritis, and other health problems. The "Ten Rules for Healthy Eating" offered in Chapter 2 can help you change course and head toward good health.

This chapter of *What to Eat* provides a brief look at how you can turn "eating wrong" into "eating right," and it gives you a peek at how we got where we are today, based on my experiences in the government and out. In Chapter 2, we look at how, by following simple rules the government won't give you, you can overcome the profound changes in our foods over the last thirty years and the negative consequences for your health and well-being. Chapter 3 discusses how marketers and media, replacing mommies, have become our national nutrition nannies, brainwashing our children and many adults into believing that junk foods are crucial to social success and feeling good, and how to combat these forces to help your children learn to eat well.

Chapters 4, 5, and 6 offer a survival guide for eating in the twenty-first century. You'll find my new Guide to Healthy Eating guidelines for eating out and on the go, and a week's worth of fast and easy menus, meals, and recipes for hectic, time-pressured days. In Chapter 7, we explore how you can nourish your emotions and spirit along with your body, even when you think you are too busy to breathe. We may eat for the sake of our physical bodies, but we eat with our minds and emotions in order to sustain our spirits.

In Chapter 8, we consider how you can come to grips with, prevent, and overcome digestive disorders by changing what and how you eat and finding your keys to feeling well. In Chapter 9, we review the most popular diets, consider some newer research on eating and appetite, and discuss how healthy eating can take the place of dieting and lead to better health as well as a slimmer waistline.

And to wrap up, Chapter 10 helps us discover what we can do in our communities to promote better food and water for ourselves, our children, our neighbors, our families, and our world. Why are we so poorly informed about nutrition? I discovered the answers during my years in Washington. I share these experiences with the hope that they will help you to know why you, not the government or any corporate interest, are the best hope for better nutrition for all people.

Food Guides and Pyramid Schemes

Fresh out of my doctoral studies, I was teaching at NYU when the nutritionist who developed the "basic four" at USDA contacted me and asked me to consider taking over her job to develop the next food guide that would replace the basic four. I was a known critic of the old guide, so I was surprised to hear from her, a former army dietitian who was about to retire from her government position. Asked why she didn't stay long enough to develop the new guide herself, she replied, "One food guide is enough in a lifetime." She didn't explain, and I had no idea what she meant until much later, when sitting in her chair, I discovered what a hot seat she'd been in.

Food guides are a way of translating dietary recommendations for nutrients into food choices. They are the most frequently used devices for teaching about nutrition, and they have a long and proud history—the first USDA food guide was developed in 1916.

The food guides are revised periodically to reflect advances in food and nutrition research and prevalent diet-related health conditions. In the 1960s, with rising rates of heart disease, high blood pressure, stroke, and diabetes in the country, a furious debate arose in the nutrition community as to whether the basic four food groups were more of a marketing tool for food commodity groups than a useful technique for improving eating practices and protecting the public's health. My public health background convinced me that to offer advice about eating that didn't reflect prevention of the major health problems linked to diet was dangerous and misleading.

Ultimately, my family and I decided to leave New York and move to Washington because it seemed like a good place to raise our children. I didn't realize that it meant walking into the lion's den and facing challenges to my integrity and professional competence that eight years in graduate school hadn't begun to prepare me for. Although excellent in all aspects of science, nutrition, and health, my education didn't include the one element that would have been extremely useful—an introduction to politics.

Before my first day on the job, I was invited to dinner with people from the food industry who said they wanted to welcome me to Washington. Naive about the way business is done in the capital, and curious to know how these food industry executives knew I existed, I accepted the invitation. We met in a quiet, clubby steakhouse near K Street, the heart of the lobbying district.

When I walked into the dimly lit room I quickly spotted six older men seated at a long table with one place conspicuously empty. I had the immediate impression that these men with weathered faces and ample girths were used to throwing their weight around. What could they possibly want with me?

They introduced themselves and, as I recall, said they were with the Cattlemen's Association, the Grocery Manufacturers, the National Food Processors, the Meat Institute, the Dairy Council, and the Egg Board. They questioned me about my nutritional opinions: how I felt about the value of butter, eggs, meat, and cholesterol in the diet, what I thought of leading consumer advocates (whom they named), suggesting offhandedly that most of them were either socialists, gay, or anarchists and therefore not to be trusted. I doubted this and wondered why they felt the need to discredit them with me.

While they grilled me about how I thought the food guide might be changed, we ordered dinner. It felt like a test—would I order the beef or a vegetable plate? I ordered fish and they ordered supersized steaks. I knew I was being evaluated to make sure I wouldn't upset the apple cart and also warned that "heavy hitters" from the food industry would be looking over my shoulder at all times. But I was from New York and New Yorkers don't intimidate easily. If anything, they had alerted me to the challenges that lay ahead.

I began work at the Beltsville Agricultural Research Center in rural Maryland; rows of low, red brick buildings, vintage 1950s, set in the bucolic landscape of a working dairy farm. In a matter of months, I had devised a plan for creating the new food guide based on studies of population diets, research on health problems linked to food and nutrition patterns, and the newest dietary standards from the National Academy of Sciences.

I convened two expert groups representing both sides of the government's nutrition "fence," agricultural scientists who studied nutritional biochemistry and medical scientists who studied diet and chronic disease. I presented them with a series of challenges designed to move us toward what would become the premises and technical basis of the next food guide, including, for the first time, consideration of target levels for fat, sugar, sodium, fiber, calories, and trace minerals in the national food guide.

The new guide would take into account both diet-related health risks and the types of foods needed for a nutritionally adequate diet. We anticipated the pending release of a Congressional report that would have the impact of an earthquake on both the government and the food industry, implicating the USDA and other government agencies in a scientific cover-up of research showing that Americans were eating "killer diets." The *Dietary Goals for the United States* report (see www.prevention institute.org for more about this report) concluded that dietary changes were urgently needed to reduce rates of nutrition-related chronic diseases that were spiraling out of control in the United States.

Eating Right or Eating Wrong

Analytic studies gave us the number of servings from each food group needed to provide target levels of vitamins, minerals, and fiber while limiting factors implicated in disease: total fat, saturated fat, cholesterol, sugar, sodium, and calories. The calorie levels that served as the basis of the guide reflected what people said they were eating daily in national surveys, an average of 1,600 calories for women, 2,200 calories for adult men, and 2,800 calories for active men, very active women, and teenage boys. We assumed that these calorie levels were underestimates, but we knew that people would have little trouble adding more calories without the government's help, if they wanted them. People who satisfied their nutritional needs within these calorie levels were more likely to consume a nutritionally adequate diet, an improvement over the situation in most national surveys.

Our new daily food guide would include a foundation of five to nine servings of fruits and vegetables, two to three of dairy, five to seven ounces of protein foods (meat, poultry, fish, eggs, nuts, and beans), and two to three servings of whole-grain breads, cereals, pasta, or rice. The lower number of servings was for women and less active men; the higher number was for teenage boys, active men, and very active women. Five servings of vegetables and fruits could be easily satisfied by a large salad (two servings), one cup of cooked vegetables, six ounces of fruit juice, and a medium apple, a not unreasonable combination. We also suggested four tablespoons of "good" fats (olive, flaxseed, expeller cold-pressed vegetable oils) and only limited amounts of refined carbohydrates. The guide assumed fats would provide 30 percent of calories and sugars no more than 10 percent of calories.

Using computer simulations, we modeled what typical meals and snacks would look like based on the public's eating patterns. The new guide, we demonstrated, would have little or no significant negative economic impact on consumers or the food industry in terms of food expenditures. Armed with this data, we made the case for the new guide to our top agency managers, showing that there would be little or no adverse impact on the U.S. food supply or the public's eating patterns and that the guide was likely to improve the nutritional quality of diets overall. Then something bizarre happened.

When the new food guide came back from review by the office of the Secretary of Agriculture, changes had been made to it. The number of servings in the whole grains category had been altered from the original two to three to six to eleven, and the words "whole grains" were nowhere to be found. Dairy was now three to four servings, protein foods had become two to three servings, and fats, oils, and sweets to "use moderately," without further explanation.

Whole grains along with vegetables and fruits formed the nutritional core of the guide we proposed. There was good science to support that decision. Numerous studies showed that in addition to making you feel fuller on fewer calories, the fiber in whole grains and fresh fruits and vegetables reduces the risks of cancer, heart disease, diabetes, high blood pressure, and stroke. The suggested servings of whole grains in our guide recognized the unique health advantages fiber-rich foods conferred in functional nutrition as well as antioxidants. Fiber-rich foods were underrepresented in American diets, where typical grain choices were white bread, processed breakfast cereals, white pasta, hamburger rolls, pizza, bagels, doughnuts, and white rice.

Whole grains provide complex carbohydrates, fiber, B vitamins, especially folic acid, vitamin E, magnesium, and other protective substances short in many diets. Refined starches contain little or no fiber, vitamins, and minerals. Although some vitamins and minerals are added back for "enrichment" or "fortification" during processing, most are not. We hoped the emphasis on whole grains would shift consumption away from refined starch toward more nutrient- and fiber-rich whole-grain breads and cereals, brown rice, and whole-wheat pastas.

The alterations that were made to the new guide would be disastrous, I told my boss, the agency director. These changes would undermine the nutritional quality of eating patterns and increase risks for obesity and diabetes, among other diseases. No one needs that much bread and cereal in a day unless they are longshoremen or football players, and it would be unhealthy for the rest of us, especially people who are sedentary or genetically prone to obesity and diabetes. What's more, bulking up on baked goods and pasta would knock other important foods out of the diet—people won't have room for less popular fruits and vegetables, which are critical for improving nutrient levels. At stake here, I told him, was nothing short of the credibility and integrity of the USDA as a source of reliable nutrition information.

Over my objections, the alterations were included and the guide was finalized. I was told this was done in order to keep the lid on the costs of the food stamp program. Fruits and vegetables were expensive, much more expensive than breads and cereals, and the added servings of grains would, to some extent, offset the loss of nutrients from fruits and vegetables, the head of our division told me. However, the logic of that rationale escaped me.

Refined wheat products are what we called in the nutrition trade "cheap carbos," stomach-filling food preferred when other, higher quality foods are unavailable or not affordable. They do little—if anything—to boost the nutritional quality of people's diets and tend to add not only starch, but also fat and sugar to the diet. It was curious that there had been no discussion of the cost constraints of the food stamp program in any previous discussion over the many months we had been working on the guide. Intuitively, I knew I was being "played," but other than stalling and requesting additional outside reviews I felt stymied.

Later, I remembered a Pan American Health Organization (PAHO) nutrition survey I had participated in during graduate school. One of our findings was a high rate of obesity among women in a particular region of the Caribbean country we were working in that had the lowest employment and per capita income. It puzzled me that the poorest region would have the most obese people until one of the physicians on our team explained that the prevalence of obesity was consistent with what he called an "impoverished diet," too little nutritious food that caused people to feel hungry all the time, and with only cheap carbohydrates available to them, their hunger was never appeased, so they ate and ate and became fatter and fatter. Was this inflated grain recommendation, I wondered, setting us up for a third world obesity scenario in our own country?

Historically, the food guide was used to calculate the cost basis of the food stamps program. Did that mean we needed to develop two different sets of standards for nutrition, one for poor people and another for those better off, or did it mean that what was affordable in the food stamps program would determine what was best for the rest of us? Neither of these Hobson's choices could be justified on scientific or ethical grounds.

The changes that were made to the guide meant that any food product containing wheat flour, from white bread, Twinkies, Oreos, and bagels to pop toasters and Reese's Puffs, would be considered nutritionally equivalent, which was not the case. With my protests falling on deaf ears, the serving suggestions in the revised guide were incorporated into the regulations for the food stamps program, as well as the school breakfast and lunch, day care, and all other feeding programs administered by the USDA. Later, Congress set the serving amounts into legislative "stone" so it would be against the law *not* to serve the expanded number of grain servings that were in the new guide, a change that meant a financial windfall for the wheat industry.

The new rules for school lunch programs increased the amount of bread and cereal products purchased for the program by 80 percent. For children in grades K through six, it meant eight daily servings of breads, cereals, and pasta, and for grades seven through twelve, ten servings. For wheat growers, this meant an increase of 15 million bushels of wheat sold annually worth about $50 million and a retail sales boost of $350 million from additional sales of cereals, breads, and snacks. That didn't include the extra sales resulting from the government-subsidized food stamps program or revenues from the industry's own efforts to shift public consumption toward more bread, pasta, and baked goods because of the new recommendations.

Throughout the nineties, Americans increased their consumption of refined grain products from record lows in the 1970s to the six to eleven servings suggested in the new guide. Whole grains, however, continued to be underconsumed at less than one serving per person, according to analysts at USDA's Economic Research Service (ERS). Consumer surveys told us why the public was avoiding whole grains: limited ability to identify them; higher prices; perceptions of inferior taste and palatability; and lack of familiarity with whole-grain cooking methods. These information gaps were easily remedied but were not addressed by the USDA. Several years later, as the director of an NIH-sponsored multicity supermarket program, I was able to demonstrate that people were not only eager for this information, but when they had it, they readily increased their consumption of fiber-rich whole grains.

Choice of whole grains also is limited by what is available on supermarket shelves, in restaurants, and in fast-foods outlets. These barriers were worse for low-income consumers in central cities and sparsely populated rural areas where food stores and product choices are more limited and cost constraints more severe.

Whole grains remain a challenge for U.S. consumers, despite evidence that they are better nutritionally and important for preventing heart disease and certain cancers. It wasn't until the 2005 edition of the *Dietary Guidelines for the United States* that three daily servings of whole grains were recommended by the government.

In the 1980s, Americans consumed an average of one hundred forty-seven pounds of wheat flour and cereal products yearly, but by 2000 we were consuming an average of two hundred pounds, an increase of more than 25 percent. According to the USDA's food economists, that converts to a little more than 10 and a half servings of wheat products daily for each of us, the upper end of the number of servings recommended in the pyramid guide.

The work of government scientists to develop the guide in 1980 had been modified to soft-pedal health advice designed to reduce risks for chronic disease. To my knowledge, it was the first time in the hundred-year history of USDA food guides that research-based dietary advice had been so blatantly manipulated to bolster sales of agricultural products.

During the Reagan years, government programs in nutrition and public health were relegated to the "deep freeze," and century-old programs for tracking national food consumption trends were shut down. Was this to hide from public attention the alarming trends in excessive consumption of calories, fat, sugar, and other dietary factors linked to disease? The food industry has its own tracking surveys, so only American consumers were kept in the dark by these subversions.

What's Wrong with Our Food?

Processed foods made for fast-food outlets and supermarkets are missing chemicals needed by pregnant women for their fetus to develop a healthy brain, retina, and nervous system. A diet made up of these foods is likely to be poor in trace minerals, some B vitamins, dietary fiber, antioxidants, and omega-3 fatty acids, deficiencies that cause behavioral problems in children and depression in adults. In the past, our foods contained more of these essential ingredients. Today, our diets are not only lacking in these and other essentials, they also contain excessive amounts of sugar, high fructose corn syrup, salt, MSG, saturated fat, and trans-fatty acids, ingredients clinically proven to promote obesity, diabetes, high blood pressure, heart problems, and cancers, according to international researchers who have issued dramatic health warnings about the foods we are marketing to the world.

Here is an example of a recent change in regulations by the USDA to accommodate food industry demands. After years of prodding by the Frozen Potato Institute, in June 2004, the USDA reclassified french fried potatoes, even those that are batter-coated, as "fresh vegetables," arguing that a fry is no less fresh than a waxed lemon. The new regulation allows fries to be substituted for salads and vegetables in school lunch, day care, and other government-subsidized feeding programs. The frozen potato product industry is hoping that the change will help it recover from the drop in U.S. consumption of about 3 percent since 1996. A major reason for the decline is the attempt by consumers to avoid "heart-unhealthy" trans-fatty acids present in french fries along with the cancer-causing chemical acrylamide, which is also found in breakfast cereals, bakery products, and snack chips.

Swedish scientists in 2002 discovered significant amounts of acrylamide in starchy foods after high-temperature commercial frying, roasting, and baking, including the most popular American foods consumed by people of all ages. Foods with high levels included breakfast cereals, potato and corn chips, french fries, bread, rolls, pizza crust, cookies, and pastries. Levels greatly exceeded the EPA allowance for the chemical in drinking water. Another possible source of acrylamide, a potent nerve toxin and probable carcinogen that also affects male fertility, are from the residues of a widely used industrial ingredient, polyacrylamide, in pesticide formulations and soil treatments among other commercial uses. The UN has called on governments to work with their food industries to significantly lower the level of acrylamide in foods. International health agencies have urged the consumption of more antioxidant-rich fresh fruits and vegetables to mitigate the damage from this and other toxic food ingredients.

Now, USDA lunchroom managers or their vendors can plate up fries as the vegetable of choice for school lunches, not what most of us would consider a healthy meal for kids. The whole point of the school lunch program paid for with our tax dollars was to introduce children to a nutritious meal and instill healthy food habits they may not learn at home. Do we need to pay schools to teach kids to prefer french fries? The USDA seems to have lost its way under the golden arches.

Nutrition and Politics

The conflict about who calls the shots in government nutrition programs was apparent in the late sixties when *The Chemical Feast: The Nader Report on the FDA*, demonstrated that most of the information about food Americans received on national television falls outside of mainstream nutrition recommendations. Americans were given one set of rules about nutrition in schools and clinics, most often in the form of the basic four food groups, while on television, children were learning another set of rules, the "basic four fun groups:" candy and chewing gum, sugared cereals and snack foods, fast foods, and soft drinks. The corporations with the biggest advertising budgets were redefining what children, and probably a lot of adults, thought they should eat and drink, and the messages were inconsistent with health recommendations.

In 1977, the U.S. Senate Select Committee on Nutrition and Human Needs, chaired by Senator George McGovern and aided by Harvard professors and their public health graduate students, released the *Dietary Goals for the United States*, suggesting limits on the amounts and

types of protein, carbohydrates, fats, fatty acids, cholesterol, sugars, and sodium Americans should eat to reduce
risks for chronic diseases that were (and still are) the leading causes of death and illness in the United States. The
publication created a furious reaction from nutritionists,
food and agriculture scientists, and food industry leaders.

Health experts and their Congressional allies called for
the USDA to shift away from advising the public to "eat
enough" and urging them to curtail consumption of
"problem nutrients" linked to degenerative diseases. From
the USDA's food industry allies came word to hold the
line—maintain the traditional focus on healthy people and
nutritional adequacy and avoid "unproven" assertions
about diet and disease. Nutrition had finally come of age.
It was now center stage politically, embroiled in a culture
war that puts powerful lobby groups at loggerheads with
nutritionists and the USDA on the "hot seat." Was the
USDA still the "people's department," as its nineteenth-
century charter declares or has it become the food and
agribusiness's department, expected to toe the industry
line? How the USDA has handled this tug-of-war is dis-
appointing, to say the least.

The brouhaha created by the *Dietary Goals for the
United States* over the healthfulness of American diets
and the USDA's responsibility as the lead government
agency for nutrition couldn't have come at a worse time.
It was a watershed period for the American food industry.
Advances in food technology were making it possible to
create tens of thousands of new food products—an
extraordinary expansion in the number and types of foods
in the marketplace, from an average of ten thousand items
in grocery stores of the 1970s to more than fifty thousand

today. Too busy promoting the globalization of food sales, the USDA finds itself unable to subscribe to precautionary principles about eating too much.

If Americans are confused, the government has done little to relieve their confusion. Take ketchup, for example. Like french fries today, ketchup once was defined as a vegetable until the USDA, undermined by the merciless witty attacks of editorial writers and consumers, reconsidered the idea. People still break out laughing on planes and in lecture halls when they hear that I was a nutritionist with the USDA, pointedly asking if ketchup is still a vegetable in Washington. Now I say, "No, but french fries are."

Chapter 2 offers "Ten Rules for Healthy Eating" based on what nutritionists know about food and health. These rules will help you determine what advice to follow in order to create a healthy eating plan and environment for yourself and your family.

In a country where Oreos are symbolic of our innocent childhoods when we enjoyed cookies and milk, what do we say to children today about the treat (and others) that has become a nutritional time bomb?

Ten Rules for Healthy Eating

If people let the government decide what foods they eat
and what medicines they take, their bodies will soon be
in as sorry a state as are the souls of those who live
under tyranny.

—THOMAS JEFFERSON

Most of us know that we could be healthier. Tired of weight swings and mood swings and sick of stress, we want to get off the merry-go-round but we're not sure where to start or what advice to trust. If we could find a pill that would give us more energy, make us look better, and feel less depressed, we would take it. But we know that's not reality.

What if I told you that there is a way for you to feel and look better and be healthier, not by taking a dose of something or signing up for cosmetic surgery but by making key lifestyle changes? You may not see results immediately—health is a process, not a destination. But if you are willing to change the way you think about food and start putting the ten simple rules in this chapter to work in your life, you will notice improvements in how you feel in days and in your health within weeks or months, depending on the shape you're in when you start this journey.

When I tell people that they have the power to feel better and to have better health, I often see disbelief in their faces. They've probably read most of the popular books that come out each year filled with confusing information and offering breakthrough approaches to dieting and overcoming common health problems. Most people who try the latest "hot" advice ultimately drop it, opting out because of boredom, frustration, or rebellion. Trying to limit what you eat or how you live your life may work for a while, but with temptation around you all the time, eventually you are going to revert to old comfortable behaviors at least once in a while, and if you don't watch out, you may quickly find yourself right back where you started.

Another typical reaction is anger. "You're not going to tell me what to eat," some people say. "I have a right to eat anything I want to," they say, dismissing a century of research about nutrition and health until they experience a serious health problem and suddenly become eager to learn what it takes to get well.

Fear is another emotion people show. Dismal statistics about our current health crises can erode your sense of personal safety and snap you into panic and denial; you're too overwhelmed to absorb positive things you can do to protect yourself. If that's your situation, you can meet the challenge by making small, stepwise changes. By adding or exchanging one better food practice for a poorer one, you can begin to turn things around and take change in stride.

Let's face it: the human species has been making food choices for hundreds of thousands of years, almost all of them without the benefit of expert advice on what to eat and drink. The basics of eating right are both inborn and shaped by hundreds of generations of experienced eaters. Where we've gone wrong is in becoming disconnected from our food and instinctive knowledge of what's good to eat.

In the past fifty years, food has been transformed into packaged products designed by industrial engineers for long shelf life, profitability, and repeat purchases. Clues about healthful eating that we once picked up in our daily lives have been wiped away by "progress," obliterated as are most natural chemicals in food that have protected people for thousands of years, just as they protected other species of animals and plants themselves. Now, industrial farming and food processing have changed all that, and we are stuck having to learn anew what foods satisfy our palates and create health; we're relying on brand names, labels, and marketing slogans instead of tried-and-true human experience.

But after sixty years of eating "scientifically," we seem to have reached the moment of truth. The great Western experiment in reinvented food has proven itself to be a health disaster. Today, across the globe and in our own backyard, more people are fat, sick, depressed, and fatigued than at any other time in recorded history. We blame ourselves for eating too many of the wrong foods, exercising too little, and expecting too much. But when all is said and done, when more people exposed to an experimental treatment become sicker rather than healthier, and more poorly nourished rather than better nourished, we have to call that experiment a failure and stop it before it does any more harm.

It is not too late for most of us to experience better health through smarter food and lifestyle choices. No matter your age or health condition, eating right can help you feel better and start you back on the road to long-term vibrant health. The "Ten Rules for Healthy Eating" are tools to help you make these changes. So, if you're ready for renewed health and vitality, start right here with these simple, down-to-earth eating changes.

Give yourself a few weeks to incorporate these changes, and make them slowly, one change at a time. Most important: trust yourself. You will know if these rules are working for you by how you feel and whether you are adding unwanted pounds or losing them in the months ahead.

Ten Rules for Healthy Eating

1. Eat a variety of fresh fruits and vegetables.
2. Eat whole-grain pasta, rice, breads, and cereals.
3. Eat certified organic foods.
4. Eat natural fats/avoid synthetic fats.
5. Avoid refined starch and sugars.
6. Eat wild fish and meat and eggs from range-fed, antibiotic- and hormone-free animals.
7. Eat several good sources of calcium.
8. Avoid too much salt and salty foods.
9. Avoid processed and additive-rich foods.
10. Drink plenty of clean, filtered water.

You will be able to tell what eating style—a more natural and less artificial one or a more highly processed and synthetic one—meets your needs best. This is your personal program. Enjoy knowing you are in control and making choices that not only feel right but also actually make you feel better.

1. Eat a Variety of Fresh Fruits and Vegetables

Eat three to five servings of vegetables and two to four servings of fruit each day. Among the many nutritional benefits of eating fresh fruits and vegetables are vitamins, fiber, magnesium, potassium, folic acid, and natural plant chemicals (phytonutrients) that protect against many chronic health diseases and conditions. In fresh produce, more than five thousand flavonoid chemicals have been identified with antiviral, anti-inflammatory, antiallergic, antitumor, antiaging, and detoxification activities that are the body's first line of defense against disease and poisoning. The variety of fruits and vegetables you consume daily directly affects your chances of developing a heart attack, diabetes, cancer, or a brain disease such as Alzheimer's.

Cranberries contain antioxidant flavonoids and polyphenols that help relax blood vessels and protect against heart attacks. They also have been shown to have a positive effect on gum disease, ulcers, and cancer.

Other examples of disease-preventing flavonoids in foods are quercetin, found in vegetables, tea, fruit skins, red wine, and onions; xanthohumol, found in hops and beer; genistein in soy; and several compounds in garlic, green onions, and leeks. Deeply colored fruits and vegetables contain color pigments that have powerful antioxidant properties that protect against infections, inflammatory conditions, and the damaging effects of free radicals associated with cancer and aging. An example is lycopene, an antioxidant pigment that gives vegetables and fruits such as tomatoes, pink grapefruit, and watermelon their red color. Several studies suggest that eating foods rich in lycopene is associated with a lower risk of prostate cancer and cardiovascular disease.

We don't think of fruits and vegetables as builders of strong bones, but the latest research says they are. Boys who eat the most fruits and vegetables have the strongest bones, a Canadian study in the September 2005 issue of the *American Journal of Clinical Nutrition* reports. Researchers who followed a group of boys and girls over a seven-year period found that while most consumed enough dairy products, they failed to eat enough fruits and vegetables. Those who consumed 10 servings of fruits and vegetables daily wound up with significantly more calcium in their bones than those who ate less, despite eating the right amounts of dairy foods. Boys who exercised and ate more fruits and vegetables had the strongest bones of all. If you don't form strong bones in the teen years you risk brittle bones (osteoporosis) later in life.

Most North Americans don't eat enough fruits and vegetables to get the full range of protection from free radicals and toxins, which is why public health authorities are campaigning vigorously to convince us to eat more of them each day. Most Americans eat no more than two vegetables daily—french-fried potatoes and iceberg lettuce. If that's your M.O., you need to diversify for the sake of your health. Add green leafy vegetables like spinach and kale and everything in between: asparagus, broccoli, cauliflower, green beans, green peas, peppers, radishes, mushrooms, beets, celery, lentils, beans, sweet potatoes, turnips, carrots—and eat some of them raw. Choose fruits that are red, blue, black, purple, and orange, and include citrus, melons, apples, pears, and berries.

Blue, black, and red berries and dark cherries are loaded with natural anti-inflammatory chemicals that can reduce arthritis pain as effectively as aspirin without aspirin's side effects. Eat different types of fruits and vegetables each day and week; fresh, vine-ripened, locally grown produce is best—frozen the next best. Wash in cold water and use a scrub brush to remove any pesticide residues, or better yet, buy certified organic produce that's wax- and residue-free. But even organic produce should be carefully washed to remove contaminants from the soil or handling.

The twelve conventionally grown fruits and vegetables in North American markets that have the highest levels of pesticides, according to the Environmental Working Group, are apples, bell peppers, celery, cherries, imported grapes, nectarines, peaches, pears, potatoes, red raspberries, spinach, and strawberries, so be sure to buy organic if possible. The twelve fruits and vegetables lowest in pesticides are asparagus, avocados, bananas, broccoli, cauliflower, sweet corn, kiwi, mangos, onions, papaya, pineapples, and sweet peas.

How about a bowl of antioxidants for lunch? Go for the mesclun, mixed fresh greens with spicy accents of arugula, basil, and radicchio, and make a great salad dressed with sprinkles of olive oil, lemon, and salt. There are also many other greens you can eat raw or lightly cooked to get your daily antioxidant fix as well as fiber, magnesium, calcium, and folic acid, which are heart–healthy factors. Go beyond spinach and try arugula, beet greens, broccoli raab, chard, chicory, collards, dandelion greens, endive, kale, mustard greens, purslane, romaine, turnip greens, and watercress. Some have a slightly bitter edge to them, an indication of their disease–fighting contents.

Antioxidants in fruits, nuts, seeds, legumes, roots, green leaves, fresh herbs and spices, red wine, and whole grains protect against free radical damage. *Free radicals* are unstable compounds normally released during metabolism, or created by the immune system, to neutralize viruses and bacteria. They also are produced by toxic environmental conditions such as pollution, cigarette smoke, herbicides, and radiation. When too many free radicals are produced or not enough antioxidants are available to neutralize them, body tissues can be damaged.

Free radicals play a central role in virtually every major human illness, from heart disease, cancer, and many inflammatory conditions to cataracts, macular degeneration, lupus, dementia, and multiple sclerosis. The bright natural pigments in unprocessed fresh fruits and vegetables are the best source of antioxidants, but if you are concerned that you don't always have time to eat everything you need, consider a daily high–quality, broad–spectrum vitamin and mineral supplement from natural sources. Synthetics don't work as well. To find the right antioxidant supplement, ask your health–care practitioner for a recommendation or talk to the manager of the supplements section of your local health food market. Choose one appropriate for your age, sex, and health condition.

Another beneficial source of antioxidants that has demonstrated anticancer properties is green tea. Try to drink two to three cups a day to take full advantage of the tea's cancer-fighting properties. Fresh garlic is another antioxidant-rich *neutraceutical*, a natural food with medicinal properties that helps to fight cancer, lowers bad cholesterol, and may even lower your blood pressure. Use it often.

2. Eat Whole-Grain Pasta, Rice, Breads, and Cereals

Natural, unprocessed, and unrefined whole grains are nutritional storehouses. Aim for two to five servings each day. Whole grains include whole wheat, oat, rye, spelt, quinua, corn, barley, millet, buckwheat, and brown rice. They provide fiber (different types from the fiber in vegetables and fruits), B-complex vitamins, vitamins A and E, and the minerals magnesium, potassium, zinc, iron, and selenium. Bleached, soft, and fluffy white flours contain no significant amounts of nutrients and fiber unless they are added back after processing. By law a few nutrients, but not all, are required to be added back. Most can't be.

Refined carbohydrates are quickly converted to sugar and more easily stored as fat. Since whole-grain products contain balanced amounts of protein, fiber, vitamins, and minerals, they are broken down more slowly in the body and have relatively low glycemic index scores, a measure used to compare the impact of various carbohydrates on blood sugar levels.

In cultures where whole grains are traditionally eaten, rates of cancer and heart disease are much lower than in ours. This can be attributed to the bulking action of fiber on stools and the protective antioxidant activity of the natural vitamins and minerals they contain. All flours are classified according to their extraction rate. Whole wheat flour contains the whole grain and is a 100 percent extraction flour. White flour used to make white bread contains only about 75 percent of the grain and is a 75 to 80 percent extraction flour. During the Second World War in Great Britain, the extraction rate of all wheat flours was increased to about 90 percent, making all wheat products sold contain more whole grain. The result was about a 40 percent drop in deaths from heart disease and cancer, which was directly attributable to nutritional improvements from changes in wheat flour and dietary restrictions. Note: With fewer fresh fruits and veggies, better nutrition via wheat was considered key.

Buy breads, cereals, and crackers that are 100 percent whole grain with the highest fiber levels you can find. If a package's nutrition label says it's whole grain but shows little fiber (two grams or less), there really is very little whole grain in the product. Whole-grain pasta and breads have a nutty taste and are more filling and satisfying than their air-puffed counterparts that you're probably used to. Keep in mind, however, that even good grains are high in carbohydrates, which can be a problem for some people who are carbohydrate-sensitive.

3. Eat Certified Organic Foods

Organic produce tastes better and is healthier than commercially cultivated produce. They contain higher levels of vitamins C and A, antioxidants, and essential minerals such as calcium, magnesium, iron, selenium, and chromium. They are free of synthetic additives suspected of contributing to heart disease, high blood pressure, diabetes, cancer, osteoporosis, migraines, ADHD, Parkinson's, and Alzheimer's, and they have no residues from the more than five hundred chemical pesticides routinely used in conventional farming, some of which are endocrine disrupters, neurotoxins, and causes of reproductive abnormalities. They are not and cannot, by law, be made from genetically modified crops that make their own pesticides and are tolerant of additional applications of chemicals. In fact, buying certified organic produce is the only way you can avoid pesticide residues in your food unless you grow it yourself. Organic foods, unlike conventional foods, must be inspected to insure compliance with stringent certification standards.

Organically raised animals are not treated with hormones, antibiotics, and growth promoters as are conventionally raised farm animals. Organic farms cause less pollution and produce less carbon dioxide and other wastes, which is good for wildlife and the environment. Free ranging, unconfined animals distribute their wastes over larger areas, while in feedlot operations housed and penned animals produce concentrated wastes that are more likely to be harmful to us and the environment.

An objection often raised to buying organic food is higher cost. But a recent study by a naturopathic physician (Colleen Huber, "Your Family Could Be Eating Organic Food for the Same Price as Processed Foods—or Less," in the online newsletter, *eHealthy News You Can Use*, February 16, 2005, www.mercola.com) demonstrated that you can buy organic food for the same price or less than processed foods, if you buy carefully. Add up the weekly cost of buying junk foods and drinks in your household— soft drinks, snack foods, desserts, candy, and pastries—and chances are you'll find your usual food costs are much higher than you realize.

The irony is that up until about fifty years ago, organic was all we had. Once farmers started to use chemically intensive agriculture and, eventually, pesticides, hormones, steroids, genetically modified crops, irradiation, and other biotechnologies, we lost what eating is all about: health, nutrition, and safety for consumers and a way of life for farmers. Now health and safety are making us turn back to organic again, and many people are discovering that organic food tastes better and makes them feel better.

Organic food represents only about 3 percent ($116 million) of the $380 billion grocery industry today. Some analysts predict that by 2020, the majority of North American consumers will be buying organic. Most Europeans already are.

4. Eat Natural Fats/Avoid Synthetic Fats

The low-fat fad of the 1980s and 1990s had many people convinced that fats were our enemy and carbohydrates our friend. In attempting to eat healthier and stay trim, many people eliminated almost *all* fat from their diets. The result: people with brittle, aged-looking skin, hair, and nails, more infections, moodiness, *and* weight gain! People who became morbidly afraid of eating fat weren't getting enough healthy fats required for critical cellular functions, protecting the brain and nervous system, absorbing vitamins, and maintaining fertility.

A moderate amount—two to three tablespoons—of natural, healthy fats is essential daily. These include extra virgin, cold-pressed olive oil (not the highly refined light versions), avocado, butter, flaxseeds and flaxseed oil, and nuts. These fats won't harm you—in fact, they protect you from illness and help you lose weight by turning off the hormone messengers that direct fat storage, especially around your midriff, which is what happens when you trade healthy fats for unhealthy carbs. Healthy fats lower LDL ("bad") cholesterol without lowering HDL ("good") cholesterol. What's more, in cultures that eat a lot of healthy fats (such as in the Mediterranean) there are much lower rates of heart disease, stroke, and cancers. Olive oil, prominent in the Mediterranean diet, is a monounsaturated fat rich in vitamin E with a natural anti-inflammatory chemical, squalene, known to slow the formation of blood clots.

Other healthy fats needed by the body for critical cellular functions, especially in the brain and nervous system, are omega-3 fatty acids. Omega-3s, found in cold-water, wild fish such as Alaska salmon and sardines, are the reason for the recommendation to eat fish twice a week in the new U.S. dietary guidelines. Wild, ocean fish are preferable because farm-raised fish may have been genetically modified or contain contaminants and antibiotics. Eating fish a minimum of once a week can halve your risk of having a coronary, reduce the risk of heart arrhythmias and high blood pressure, improve inflammatory conditions such as rheumatoid arthritis, and protect against common cancers. Research shows that omega-3 fatty acids also mitigate or prevent some psychiatric disorders, including depression, bipolar disorder, and schizophrenia.

Omega-3 fatty acids are believed to slow down the aging process, and they have been shown to improve Alzheimer's and Parkinson's as well as other chronic neurological conditions associated with free radical damage. Plant sources of omega-3 fatty acids include almonds, walnuts, flaxseeds, and flaxseed oil. In addition to eating wild, fatty fish twice a week, it's a good idea to take up to two tablespoons of flaxseed oil or organic, descented, high-quality fish oil daily, and to nibble on nuts—especially almonds and walnuts. *Moderate amounts of natural fats combined with a balance of saturated, polyunsaturated, and monounsaturated fats from natural foods—even those containing cholesterol—are needed and contribute to functional health!* Too much biologically unstable polyunsaturated and synthetic fats like trans- and hydrogenated fats is more dangerous for the heart and neurovascular system than any other kind. Natural fats, including olive oil, butter, and nuts, are stable and don't create dangerous levels of free radicals in the body, interfere with immunity, or block blood vessels. This is different than what conventional medical authorities tell us; however, there is a rich research literature that backs up the healthfulness of traditional fats, which have been used for thousands of years and include cold-pressed olive oil, flax and fish oils, butter, and animal fats. Problem fats have been eaten for a much briefer time in human evolution and include hydrogenated oil, high polyunsaturated oils such as soy, corn, and safflower, cottonseed oil, canola oil, and all fats heated to very high temperatures in processing and frying. For a comprehensive discussion of this subject, visit the Weston A. Price Foundation site at www.westonaprice.org/index .html.

Avoid hydrogenated fats, which are implicated in heart disease because they cause arteries to become more rigid and clogged, which raises LDL (bad) cholesterol levels and creates conditions for heart attacks. Good saturated fats are found in meats, poultry, eggs, butter, cheese, ice cream, and other whole milk products containing milk fat such as coffee drinks, creamy sauces, and desserts. Hydrogenated fats are damaged fats that have been altered through processing. They contain trans-fatty acids, "backwards" fatty acids that are not found in nature. Our bodies can't metabolize trans-fatty acids so they accumulate, clogging arteries and cells and causing inflammation, cell damage, and heart attacks. Hydrogenated fats are in deep-fried foods, margarine, baked goods, artificial creamers, and many other foods. Check labels for the words *hydrogenated* or *partially hydrogenated*. Also avoid commercial high heat–processed vegetable oils made of corn, soy, and canola. Most commercial soy and canola oils are made from genetically modified ingredients and may contain toxic ingredients and/or be altered in processing. Our bodies don't handle them well and they don't offer the health advantages of natural fats or cold-pressed vegetable oils.

5. Avoid Refined Starch and Sugars

Limit sweetened foods and drinks to no more than 10 percent of daily calories. Foods made with refined white flour that are heavily sweetened with sugar or corn (or high fructose) sweeteners are digested rapidly, which releases large amounts of glucose into your bloodstream quickly. This triggers the release of insulin and other hormones that convert excess sugar into fat (the kind that is stored around your middle) to push it out of your bloodstream and normalize your blood sugar level. Refined starch and sugars not only make you fatter but also cause common sugar-related diseases, from metabolic syndrome, high blood pressure, and high blood sugar levels to hypoglycemia and hyperinsulinemia, which is often associated with metabolic syndrome—insulin accumulates because it is not being effectively used. The body of a person with metabolic syndrome not only can't use insulin effectively but also tends to have high blood cholesterol and triglyceride levels that can lead to type 2 diabetes.

Artificial sweeteners are not the answer, as the brain tends to register them like regular sweeteners, releasing the same fat-making hormones. Sugars are also blamed for contributing to high triglyceride levels (one of the bad blood fats), cavities, and candida (yeast problems).

Be careful about consuming concentrated sweets like soft drinks that contain up to twelve teaspoons of sugar in a single serving. The bloodstream normally holds only about two teaspoons of sugar (glucose) at one time. When twelve more teaspoons of sugar are dumped into your bloodstream all at once, biochemical and hormonal chaos are the result.

Complex carbohydrates in fruits, vegetables, whole grains, and dairy products, on the other hand, are broken down slowly and diffuse into the bloodstream more gradually without triggering fat-making hormones. High levels of refined carbohydrates also trigger the release of enzymes associated with inflammatory responses. So choose your carbohydrates carefully, and don't be fooled into thinking that anything labeled low-fat, "low net carbs," or carb-controlled is good for you. Less-refined carbs are better for most people who are not athletes or high metabolic burners.

Most artificial sweeteners, as mentioned earlier, are unfortunately not a good substitute for sugars. Sweeteners including aspartame (NutraSweet), acesulfame-K, saccharin, and sucralose are associated with behavioral problems, hyperactivity, allergies, and possibly cancers; the government cautions against the use of any artificial sweetener by children and pregnant women. Anyone with PKU (phenylketonuria) should not use aspartame (Nutra-Sweet), which is an excitotoxin damaging to brain and nerve cells.

6. Eat Wild Fish and Meat and Eggs from Range-Fed, Antibiotic- and Hormone-Free Animals

Consume a total of five to eight ounces of protein foods daily, with seafood at least twice a week. You need protein even when you are trying to lose weight. In fact, eating more protein and fewer carbohydrates may help you lose weight more efficiently. Try to eat at least a small amount of protein (one or two ounces) in every meal and snack. Choose lean poultry and meats. Toxins are stored in the fatty skin and tissues of animals (as they are in our bodies), so you will consume fewer toxins *and* fewer calories when you choose leaner protein foods. Wild fish from the sea are preferable to farm-raised fish because they are less likely to contain heavy metals and pesticide residues, and they are less likely to be genetically modified.

Seafood is a good source of lean protein and also is low in saturated fat, which can be helpful for individuals with heart disease or diabetes, who need to maintain moderate saturated fat levels.

A valuable source of omega-3 fatty acids are found mainly in cold-water, fatty fish such as salmon, tuna, sardines, rainbow trout, mackerel, herring, and anchovies. The risks of eating seafood should be considered along with the benefits. Fish and shellfish take in harmful substances in the food they eat, including heavy metals (methylmercury) and organic chemicals such as DDT and dioxin. The bottom line: eat wild fish, but limit the amount of large fish, such as tuna or swordfish, to two times a month. Big fish accumulate more methylmercury and other toxins than smaller, younger fish, which can safely be eaten more often. Check with your doctor if you are concerned about eating fish when you're pregnant or feeding a young child.

Mercury from industrial pollution settles on the surface of water and bacteria transforms it into methylmercury, a highly toxic substance. Fish consume the toxic material when they feed on aquatic organisms, and the larger fish accumulate the most methylmercury and store it in muscle tissue, which is why several national advisories have been issued recently to caution against eating tuna and swordfish too often.

Other industrial toxins include organochlorines, DDT, PCBs, and dioxins, which, although banned decades ago, persist in the air, water, and soil and still are found in the fatty tissue of both marine and land animals. Humans accumulate these substances in their fatty tissues primarily by consuming animal fats. In adults, exposure to mercury can cause memory loss, tremors, and may lead to higher risks for certain cancers. But children and pregnant women are the most vulnerable to the damaging health effects of these toxins.

The Environmental Defense Fund's list of the best seafood choices for health and the environment includes abalone, Arctic char, catfish, clams, crabs, halibut, herring, mackerel, oysters, Alaskan salmon, mahi mahi, mussels, scallops, shrimp (U.S. farmed), striped bass, and tilapia.

Other protein choices are beans, eggs, nuts, seeds, and nut butters. One-half cup of cooked dry beans or lentils, one egg, or two tablespoons of peanut butter count as one ounce of lean meat or fish. Dry beans and lentils count as both protein and vegetables; so be sure to count them in only one group. Cheese is another crossover food counted in the dairy and protein groups. Most cheeses are heat-treated or aged, which can damage the fat they contain, so use them sparingly. White cheeses tend to have the least fat and are the healthiest choices. They include cottage cheese, feta, goat cheese, mozzarella, ricotta, Neufchâtel, and queso fresca. Count them as a protein or a calcium food choice.

It's best to buy your meat fresh and cook it within a day. Fresh meat two or more days old has begun to oxidize and contains free radicals. If you can't buy fresh, look for high-quality frozen organic or range-fed meats and poultry now available in many supermarkets and on the Internet. Cook proteins at low to moderate temperatures to avoid damaging the fat they contain, which is less of a problem when you select lean, organic meats to begin with.

Make sure to avoid packaged, smoked, additive- and nitrate-preserved fish and luncheon and deli meats. Some smoked ham and bacon are cured with sugar and are nitrate-free, but the smoke and chemical residues they contain are toxic, so eat them sparingly.

7. Eat Several Good Sources of Calcium

Children and teens need two to three servings of calcium-rich foods each day; adults need one to two servings. Good sources of calcium include dishes made with milk or cheese, such as puddings, soups, pizza, melted cheese sandwiches, and yogurt; canned fish (sardines or salmon) with soft bones; leafy greens such as kale, mustard greens, turnip tops, and bok choy; tofu (if made with calcium sulfate); and tortillas made with lime-processed corn. Read each ingredient and nutrition label to ensure that the foods provide at least 150 mg of calcium per serving and include other nutrients as well.

8. Avoid Too Much Salt and Salty Foods

Americans consume twice as much salt daily as is recommended by leading health experts. According to the Center for Science in the Public Interest (CSPI), too much salt—or to be more accurate—too much sodium, the part of salt implicated in high blood pressure, heart attacks, and strokes, kills about 150,000 Americans each year. About 65 million Americans have hypertension (high blood pressure) and another 50 million are prehypertensive. Too much sodium over a lifetime puts your life at risk.

The 2005 edition of the government's *Dietary Guidelines for Americans* recommends that young people eat less than 2300 mg of sodium daily, and African-Americans, middle-aged, and elderly people eat no more than 1500 mg a day. Your sodium level depends on how many commercial foods and "take out" meals you eat—80 percent of the sodium in our diets comes from processed and restaurant foods. The salt shaker on your table only contributes about 10 percent of your daily intake.

Thousands of processed foods contain between 500 and 1000 mg of sodium per serving. About 1400 mg are found in instant Ramen noodles, which fulfills an entire day's recommended servings; a Denny's Lumberjack breakfast can have as much as 4500 mg; and a Chinese entrée of General Tao's chicken can contain 3150 mg, reports the CSPI. And, to top it off, no two brands of the same food have the same amount of sodium. Read the labels—it is the only way you'll know if the "light" salad dressing you like has 600 mg of sodium or just 170. Ask your favorite restaurant for the sodium levels of their foods. You may not get it, but it might trigger them into getting it. In Britain, American food manufacturers (Heinz, Kraft, McDonald's) have reduced the sodium content of their foods in response to a government campaign to reduce sodium consumption by one-third. Why isn't our government doing the same? Probably because they don't think you know enough to care.

You can drop your sodium level by reading labels and buying more carefully, but also by eating fewer commercial foods and restaurant meals and eating more fresh fruits and vegetables, which contain very little sodium.

9. Avoid Processed and Additive-Rich Foods

There are other additives besides sodium that deserve our attention and should be used with caution. Read ingredient labels on packaged foods to check for the following risky additives:

- **Artificial food colors.** Food coloring has been linked to allergies, asthma, hyperactivity, and possibly some cancers.
- **Nitrates.** These chemicals can form nitrosamines, a highly carcinogenic compound, in the body. Nitrates are chemical preservatives used in ham, hot dogs, bacon, sausage, and luncheon meats and are formed in charbroiled meats and smoked fish.
- **Sulfites (sulfur dioxide).** Associated with allergic reactions and asthma. You'll find sulfites, used as preservatives, in wine, shrimp, salad bar veggies (unless posted otherwise), fast-food fries, and other restaurant fare. If you have asthma or know you are sulfite-sensitive, ask if there are sulfites in or on foods before you order. An emergency trip to the hospital is not a pleasant ending to a dinner out.

- **MSG (monosodium glutamate).** In hundreds of studies conducted by scientists around the world, rats have been injected with MSG to make them obese. These MSG-treated rats are used as test subjects in diabetes and diet research. In these studies, MSG triples the amount of insulin produced by the pancreas, causing obesity in the rats. MSG probably does the same in humans. And, MSG is not only found in Chinese restaurant food. It's in everything from Doritos, potato chips, Ramen noodles, and hamburger helper to canned soups, frozen TV dinners, salad dressings, bouillon cubes, and steak sauce.

   On food labels it is listed as MSG, "hydrolyzed vegetable protein," Accent, natural meat tenderizer, and Aginomoto. It is widely used in menu items served by fast food restaurants, including Burger King, McDonalds, Wendy's, Taco Bell, Chili's, Applebees, Denny's, and Kentucky Fried Chicken. It is added to food for the addictive effect it has on our bodies. If you can't eat just one of something, look for MSG as an ingredient on the label and you'll understand why.
- **Food preservatives.** Preservatives, including BHA, BHT, and EDTA, are linked to allergy and sensitivity reactions from mild rashes and hives to GI upsets and anaphylactic reactions, hyperactivity, and possibly cancer. BHT may be toxic to the nervous system and the liver.
- **Synthetic flavors.** Chemical flavorings have been associated with allergic reactions and behavioral problems in children.
- **Food waxes.** The protective coating on produce such as cucumbers, peppers, and apples contains pesticides, fungicides, and animal byproducts that can

trigger an allergic reaction. Fruits and vegetables can be coated with food-grade animal-based wax or food-grade vegetable-, petroleum-, beeswax-, and/or shellac-based wax or resin to maintain freshness.

- **Plastic packaging.** May contain vinyl chloride that can increase your risk for cancer, immune reactions, and lung problems.
- **Heat-processed soy.** This form of soy is a common food allergen suspected of causing breast and other hormone-related cancers, suppressing thyroid function, and causing problems with protein digestion and mineral absorption, male infertility, and decreased sex drive.
- **Genetically modified foods.** Biotechnology uses the technique of genetic engineering to redesign life forms to satisfy the demands of the marketplace. But these techniques of splicing DNA from unrelated plants, animals, and microbes to the cells of our foods have been introduced to the market untested, and unanticipated consequences from these methods can not only endanger consumers, but potentially, all life on earth. Today, more than 80 percent of the soy ingredients in our foods have been genetically engineered while at the same time allergies to soy have increased 50 percent. Some scientists urge caution and worry about the potential for weakening people's immune systems, while others point to damaging effects seen in animal studies. The government continues to encourage the use of these unproven techniques in foods without labeling or otherwise identifying them. The only way to avoid them is by eating certified organic foods, exclusively.

10. Drink Plenty of Clean, Filtered Water

The most abundant essential substance your body needs is water. Seventy percent of our bodies are made up of water, and all the chemical reactions continuously underway in our tissues and cells must take place in a watery environment. You've probably had the experience of feeling very tired as the day wore on and realizing that you had very little to drink all day. If you solved the problem by downing several good-sized gulps of water, you probably felt less tired afterward. But what's better is making sure you have a continuous supply of water all day. Make a habit of drinking six to eight glasses of water each day. Don't wait until you feel thirsty because that is a late signal of your body's need for water replacement.

If you live in an urban area and have a municipal water system that pipes water into your home, your water probably has been treated with disinfectants (chlorine), and additives (fluoride) that are toxic, and may also contain traces of industrial wastes such as lead or mercury. Fluoride, which is added to the water supply because it is believed to help prevent dental cavities, is a known thyroid toxin, a neurotoxin, and a cause of periodontal disease and, possibly, of brittle bones and bone cancer in young men. There is some evidence that topical application of fluoride to children's teeth might be more effective and less risky for people of all ages who drink fluoridated water. Toxins get into water systems from many sources including farm and factory runoff, acid rain, and plastic and metal ions dissolved from pipes. Government inspectors usually test water only for bacterial contamination, lead, and arsenic. You can have your water tested by an outside lab for a more complete look at what you are exposed to.

Bottled water may or may not be cleaner than tap water, depending on where it comes from and how it's been handled. If you are going to use bottled water, ask to see an analysis of it and be sure it tastes good. Off tastes can indicate dissolved plastics or waste products in the water.

Installing your own water filtering system is cheaper than buying filtered water. The two best are steam distillation systems (which are more expensive) and reverse osmosis systems in which water is passed through a semipermeable membrane that is a barrier to contaminants. Filters have to be changed periodically; make sure you know how often they need changing.

Other Health-Promoting Habits

In addition to following the "Ten Rules for Healthy Eating," there are other habits you can acquire that will promote good health, which include eating moderate portion sizes, exercising daily, getting enough sleep, and using fresh herbs and spices often and natural supplements as needed.

Eat Moderate Portion Sizes

Don't diet. Instead, develop a new mind-set based on eating the right foods and occasionally enjoying other foods you like in modest amounts. Become committed to permanent changes that get you to your weight goals slowly, over time. That type of weight loss is more likely to be lasting. Eat enough fiber-rich vegetables, fruits, whole grains, dairy, and protein foods to avoid feeling hungry or unsatisfied, and stay away from "trigger" foods and drinks (concentrated sweets, greasy foods, breads and pastries made with white flour, alcohol, cola drinks, juices) that just make you want to eat more. You won't have to avoid foods you love or starve all day so you can binge at dinner, and you'll be creating good health moment by moment.

Be aware that low-fat, low-quality diets high in processed foods are eroding your health. You need natural foods, not synthetic ones, when you're trying to cut down. Your insatiable appetite for favorite snack foods (popcorn, chips, or chocolate covered raisins) may just be a sign that your body is missing something it needs, not cookies, but a nutrient or dietary essential.

Avoid stress eating. Stress prompts the release of hormones that encourage the storage of fat around the midsection, slows metabolism, and endangers the heart.

Exercise Daily

Energy needs vary by age, size, and stage of life. Older adults need less food than younger, more active people. But if you are too sedentary and trying to lose weight, you may have to cut down on what you eat so much that you eat too little and not only fail to lose weight because your metabolism has dropped down to starvation mode, but you won't be getting all the nutrition you need to stay well and energized. A better approach is to increase your "burn rate."

To up the ante on the calories your body burns, try to walk briskly for at least a half hour daily, and several times weekly also do some resistance training or weight-bearing exercises followed by stretching. You need a variety of exercises each week to stay trim, fit, and flexible. Vary the experiences with the weather and enjoy the outdoors whenever possible.

Get Enough Sleep

People who don't get enough sleep have a harder time losing weight and keeping it off. When you go without or get too little sleep your body produces less growth hormone, which is needed to control your body's ratio of muscle to fat, as well as less leptin, the hormone that controls how much we eat and tells us when we are full. When we are sleep-deprived, the reduction of leptin makes us crave carbohydrates, even when we've eaten enough calories. Unless we burn the extra carbs, they're converted to fat and stored in our bodies.

Use Fresh Herbs and Spices Often and Natural Supplements as Needed

Enjoy eating a variety of fresh, nourishing, wholesome, and unadulterated foods. Will it help you to be healthier, slimmer, and more relaxed? You bet! What we eat has everything to do with our state of health and mind. Our challenge is to transcend the assumptions we've grown up with based on what we've learned from doctors, advertising and promotion by food companies, and the industry-friendly guidance of the government. Real food is a real alternative, if you know where to look.

Real food connects us to each other and to the earth. Our need for nourishment is a common human imperative that binds us together and reminds us of our joint human heritage. Disease and premature death have been with us for a long time. Despite our advances in science and technology, they are flourishing today, not because we don't have enough food to feed us all but because our foods are less nutritious and more denatured with each passing year.

Herbs and spices are good medicine: a natural, green pharmacy of safe, time-honored, natural remedies for everything from asthma (anise) and diabetes (cinnamon) to memory boosting (rosemary), migraines (bay leaf), and toothaches (clove). When you start to feel ill with a cold, flu, or infection, you may need to take additional supplements for a short time to speed your recovery. Do your homework searching the Internet and talking to knowledgeable people to come up with ideas for natural antioxidant herbs, teas, and remedies that have antibacterial or antiviral activity or help you to heal from minor health problems. For more information about herbs and natural remedies go to the following websites:

- American Botanical Council (www.herbalgram.org)
- American Holistic Medical Association (AHMA) (www.holisticmedicine.org)
- Naturopathic Medicine Network (www.panda medicine.com)

If you are interested in wellness, you already know that your health is worth the price of the best food choices you can make. You may even have become a nutrition vigilante, someone who knows the difference between faux food made in a factory and the original made by nature and is actively spreading the word. Practical, independent people always opt for the real McCoy, even if it takes a while to see the light through the fog of false and misleading marketing claims. Nutrition is not a matter of purchasing food products that manufacturers promote as healthy, but of choosing foods that have proven their merit over many generations.

In Chapter 3, we consider the plight of children as the target of junk food marketing at home, in school, and at the mall and offer strategies and insights for creating a healthy food environment for healthier kids.

Kids—Hungry for Change

The tsunami of childhood obesity has not yet hit the shore. It takes many years for complications to develop. If the clock starts ticking at age twelve or fourteen, the consequences to public health are potentially disastrous.

—David Ludwig, M.D., Children's Hospital, Boston

Children grow up eating healthy despite erratic eating habits, a controversial study from the 1920s showed. Confirmed by researchers from the University of Illinois in 1991, children will choose nutritious foods when given healthy choices and enough time. Even the author of the most trusted handbook for parents ever published, Dr. Benjamin Spock, was confident that parents could instill sound nutrition practices in their children. His food and eating advice, first published in 1945, guided many generations of parents and is still valid today, "Parents should insist that children take at least the following foods daily: a pint of skimmed milk, meat or poultry or fish, a green or yellow vegetable, fruit twice, and three or four eggs a week, in reasonable servings." Dr. Spock warned that rich desserts should be avoided, and the amount of starchy foods would determine how much weight a child gains or loses.

More than half a century later that advice seems quaint because fast food, junk food, and soft drinks have become an integral part of growing up, with the number of food ads directed at children skyrocketing and portion sizes as well as body weights ballooning. Child obesity has climbed 50 percent in each of the previous two decades, with the largest increases seen in children who spend most of their time watching television and using computers.

The consequences of our obesity-inducing culture, according to Dr. David Ludwig, author of a scathing report on the subject in the 2005 volume of the *New England Journal of Medicine*, are unprecedented health dangers facing the current generation of children, from type 2 diabetes to premature heart attacks, which we used to think of as exclusively adult diseases, as well as shortened lives.

Ludwig reports that:

- One soft drink per day increases a child's risk of obesity by 60 percent.
- Ninety percent of preschoolers drink at least one sweetened soft drink daily and 40 percent drink three a day.
- Fifty percent of school districts have contracts with soft drink companies giving them exclusive "pouring rights" to sell their drinks on school grounds.
- Thirty percent of all children eat fast food every day.

- A single fast-food meal contains 100 percent of rec-ommended total daily calories but limited amounts of essential nutrients.
- The average child watches thirty thousand food ads annually.
- The bill for children's food advertising is $15 billion a year, most of it for sugary, starchy, and nutritionally poor products.
- Each hour of TV a child watches raises his or her risk for obesity by 12 percent.
- Each hour of exercise decreases the risk of obesity by 10 percent.

Foods marketed to children have become a major health concern. Research shows that as much as one-third of children's diets consist of foods low in nutritional value and heavy on calories, like intensely sweetened soft drinks and greasy, salty snacks. Soft drinks alone account for 7 percent of many children's daily calories, about the same amount as that contributed by fruits and vegetables, according to government surveys.

Community schools peddle junk food to children, and the government supports and defends junk food mar-keters. What would Dr. Spock say to parents today whose kids have been recruited into an army of "kid culture" ambassadors promoting cool foods, clothing, and acces-sories as essential to social success and happiness? What can a parent do about kid marketing campaigns that push soda pop and other sweet drinks, cookies, and other "fun foods" that children find irresistible even though they play havoc with their waistlines, emotions, energy levels, and thought processes? Children are impressionable targets for food advertisers, but there are things you can do to protect them. The ultimate decision about whether to buy into the junk food culture is made by you as parent, grandparent, friend, and neighbor. You still can provide a powerful, positive influence on children's eating habits.

Your children learn what's good to eat from what you eat, serve, stock in your cupboard and refrigerator, and buy in the grocery store. They may protest, pester, go on an occasional hunger strike, or indulge in junk food when you're not around, but in the end they will learn to prefer the tastes and textures of the foods they grow up eating. If you doubt this, I have a story for you.

When my oldest daughter, Sara, came back home for the summer after her first year away at college, she made some requests. "Please have some white foods for me, not just grainy brown ones, and some good snacks." What she meant was for me to buy junk foods for her like those she ate at college, and not to expect her to eat healthy foods like the ones she grew up with.

I felt crushed, a failure as a parent. All my good nutrition intentions had been for naught. But an inner voice told me not to give up and to persevere in buying the foods the rest of the family prefer. If Sara wants to eat differently and you don't agree with it, you don't have to become a codependent coconspirator. Buy what you buy and eat what you eat.

When I explained to my daughter why she wouldn't find the white foods and sweet snacks she requested, she stormed out, intimating that she might spend the summer with friends elsewhere! Our compromise was that she could buy what she liked out of the house, but at home, house rules prevailed. We made our peace, and the good news is that today she is a paragon of healthful eating, committed to it in her life and with her family. She even teaches it!

Not eating right has long-term negative consequences. Children deficient in basic nutrition exhibit increased aggressive behavior. A study in the *American Journal of Psychiatry* (2005) showed that eight-year-olds short on zinc, iron, and B vitamins—essential for a healthy nervous system—demonstrate 40 percent more aggressive behavior than those without these deficiencies, and seventeen-year-olds were 50 percent more violent and presented with antisocial behaviors.

Zinc is the single most common nutritional deficiency in North America, with 80 percent of the population believed deficient. Other side effects of poor zinc nutrition are weakened immune systems, impaired wound healing, reduced sexual potency in males, and poor fetal development in pregnant women. Refined white flour and sugar are devoid of zinc and deplete the body of B vitamins. In the developing world, the major source of zinc and B vitamins are whole-grain breads and cereals, foods unfamiliar and unpopular with most North American children.

If I've convinced you that the food choices your children make are not a trivial matter, here are some things you can do to create in them an appetite for change.

Limit TV

Viewing too many hours of television not only overexposes your children to commercials that promote poor nutrition but also encourages them to be couch potatoes.

Instead, encourage your kids to participate in sports, exercise, and physically active play. Set limits on how much television they can watch each week and reward them with nonfood treats for sticking to the schedule, such as the concert they want to see or a membership at a kid-friendly local gym.

The influence of food advertising is pernicious, taking root when you're least aware. One of the worst culprits is breakfast cereals advertised as good for kids although they are nutritionally inferior: overprocessed grains with too many calories from highly refined flour, sugar, and artificial food colors and flavors, with all their "good nutrition" coming from the few synthetic nutrients added back after they've been processed out. A good example is General Mills' Shrek cereal, which uses a popular cartoon character to sell cereal with fourteen grams of sugar per serving, as much as in a McDonalds chocolate chip cookie. Is breakfast cereal that resembles a cookie or candy really the best choice for starting the day? After you answer that one, check out soda pop, which is liquid candy. Did you know that kids in North America drink an average of two times more soda than milk?

Set a Good Example

I will never forget the lesson I learned from a series of focus group studies I worked on at the U.S. Department of Agriculture. The purpose was to gain insight into how to increase children's fruit eating and decrease their candy consumption. Mothers in the groups talked at length about how worried they were about their children's poor eating habits while nibbling on candy from a big bowl on the table.

When you give children a double message, "Eat what I say, not what I do," you undercut your authority and give them permission to eat what you do, not what you say. Instead of hiding your own very human struggles making the right choices, talk about it with your kids. It's a struggle for most people. Talking about it gives you a chance to say why you believe it's so important and worth the struggle. The important thing is not to give up but to keep trying. Research shows that if you don't give up, you will eventually succeed.

If you have a pet at home, your children will learn why it's important to feed the pet the right foods, not junk, and to make sure the pet is getting enough exercise. Pets don't watch TV, but they pick up our sedentary habits, so you and your kids need to set a good example for them. Once kids understand that what they put in their mouths bears a direct relation to how they feel, think, and look, just as it does with the family pet, they may be ready to eat right.

However, kids also pick up a lot of half-baked ideas from other kids, from their own perceptions of what's "in," and what might make them more popular. Most of these ideas are innocuous, but not all of them are harmless. There's a blurry line between nutritionally okay behaviors and risky ones that can lead to serious eating problems. Watch for any sudden changes in your child's food behavior and start a conversation about it. If you look closely and stay in touch with what's going on, you can prevent a world of trouble. But you have to look at yourself, too.

Use these questions for guidance. If you answer yes to any of them, you may be enabling the very food behaviors you are trying to discourage. Are you:

- Telling your kids to clean their plates?
- Serving overlarge food portions?
- Drinking soft drinks and eating potato chips yourself?
- Starving your body to be thin?
- Avoiding fresh fruits and vegetables?
- Stopping for quick meals at fast-food restaurants?
- Keeping junk food on hand as emergency nibbles?
- Not reading nutrition labels?
- Not stocking enough fresh fruits and vegetables in the house?
- A pizza, hamburger, and fried chicken fan?
- Staying away from fats and eating more carbs?
- A sucker for heat-and-serve convenience foods?
- Buying the sugary, greasy, processed food your child begs for?

It's not easy being a mom or dad, but the ultimate decision on whether to buy junk food is up to you. Becoming aware of the ways you contribute to the problem can help protect your children from the most obtrusive methods used by junk food marketers who drown kids in unhealthy messages.

You can't shelter your children from every brand of food identified with a celebrity, cartoon character, or sports star, but you can help them understand why relying solely on ads as the basis for their nutrition will get them into trouble. Recognize that children under the age of eight, according to the American Psychological Association, tend to accept advertising messages uncritically, so you may have to make some decisions for them and reinforce them by what you do.

A study from Appalachian State University in North Carolina showed that when mothers add more fruits and vegetables to their plates, their daughters do as well. What's more, moms who eat lots of fruits and veggies are less likely to pressure their daughters to eat more, and their daughters are less likely to become "picky" eaters. The researchers say the same trends are not seen with young boys because parents don't worry as much about boys' weight.

Stock the Good Stuff

Those who do the household shopping have a mental picture of where things go in the kitchen. You probably have special places for bottles and cans, bags of chips and goodies, canned soups and tuna, spices and condiments, tea and coffee, pasta, cooking oils, and so on. Draw a picture of your pantry area and label the shelves you use for storing various kinds of provisions. Now look down the list and check off the shelves with nutritionally poor products, from cookies, snacks, and candy to soft drinks and sugared cereals, as well as products high in sugars (both caloric and noncaloric), salt, artificial additives, trans- and hydrogenated fats, and modified starch. You may have to check the nutrition and ingredient labels to find out which ones they are. Now decide if you and your family can live without these items. If you think you can, it's time to junk the junk food.

Have a family conference about it before you take action. If you can get family members to agree, bag up the junk food and donate it to your local emergency feeding center. Then go shopping to replace the items you've given away with more nutritious ones: nuts and seeds, whole-grain crackers and biscuits, canned beans and bean pastes, olive oil, club soda and bottled water, and fresh foods high in nutrition and low in artificial chemicals—real foods that contain natural vitamins, minerals, and antioxidants that your family needs. If you think this is too costly a solution, consider the cost of treatment for your child for diet-related diseases such as obesity, asthma, food allergies, childhood diabetes, and cancer. Believe me, fresher, healthier foods are less risky and the better bargain!

You'll be surprised at how much more room you have and how easy it is to find things now! But best of all, you'll know that you are providing healthy alternatives to the unhealthy ones you and your family have been hooked on. Your family may even surprise you and ask for more fresh and fewer factory foods because they taste better and make them feel better. This is a call for you to increase the amount of local, unprocessed, and organic ingredients in your menus. Meals made with more whole, natural ingredients and fresh fruits and vegetables are richer in vitamins and minerals and less full of salt, sugar, starch, and "bad" fats.

You can do a lot as a parent, but you can't do it all. In addition to food ads, peer pressure, and foods eaten at home, the most important influence on your children's eating habits are what they eat at school. In the United States, we have more and better food available for more people than ever before, but we love "cheap eats," and we graze all day long. Vending machines and convenience foods make grazing possible—even in our public schools.

Federal food programs including meals for schoolchildren cost $46 billion a year. The foods featured in these meals are powerful marketing tools for the food industry that, in the past, has used the federal school meals programs to market and test new food products. Advertising and promotion companies with strong ties to food companies design icons used to help Americans interpret federal nutrition advice. Do subtle messages in the government's food guides designed by these marketers give the edge and millions of dollars' worth of sales to favorite processed food companies? There is a history that says they do.

In the 1980s, the original food guide pyramid was scheduled for release by the U.S. Department of Agriculture but was stopped because of complaints by the milk and meat producers that the placement of their products in the food pyramid might discourage people from eating their products. Grain producers objected to fruits and vegetables making up the base of the pyramid and succeeded in having grains replace them. The government's first dietary guidelines pamphlet was published at that time, but only after the meat producers succeeded in coercing the government to change the color associated with meat from red to dark purple because red was too closely identified with meat in the public's eye. The producers worried that red would mean stop or no to people and focus their attention on meat as "bad." The food guide pyramid was finally released in the 1990s, but it has-n't done much toward improving dietary habits. Although 80 percent of the public recognize the food pyramid, only a negligible number actually use it to guide their eating decisions; meanwhile, the rate of overweight and obesity has skyrocketed.

The USDA has come out with a kid version of My Pyramid.com that avoids telling them to eat less of any-thing, including soft drinks, candy, fast food, potato chips, and the rest of the junk foods in supermarkets and vend-ing machines. Studies in the *American Journal of Public Health* show how the deck has been stacked against parents by food marketers who aggressively target kids using incentive programs (toy giveaways, tie-ins to favorite car-toon characters, and cross-marketing with kids' movies). The Government Accountability Office in 2005 reported on the saturation of schools with junk foods and USDA's failure to get things right. Is the new kid version of My Pyramid.com yet another case of "let them eat cake" by government officials who zealously protect the rights of marketers at the expense of our kids and real national nutrition improvement? If you don't accept this appalling state of affairs, it's time to tell our elected leaders to put our money where it will do children the most good.

A Big Revolution

In Britain, a program by popular TV chef Jamie Oliver exposed some of the mystery foods dished up daily to schoolchildren in that country. His programs have created a furor among parents who want better school meals for their children. A national movement has sprung up to swap junk food served in schools for more nutritious meals and snacks made with organic, local ingredients.

In response to the uproar over the quality of school meals, the British government is cooking up "One of the biggest revolutions that England has ever seen," says chef Oliver. Kitchens and dining areas are being revamped, teachers are working with parents to develop proper nutrition standards for bag lunches brought from home, and parent petitions are demanding low-fat, healthy, and fresh school food and a curb on junk food TV advertising to young children.

The key to this revolution is not more money spent on school meals but better recipes, ingredients, and cooking methods. "The world is not short of recipes. What matters are the ingredients and how food is cooked and served," says Michelin-starred chef Shaun Hill. What sounds wonderful on a menu can taste like nothing when it's plated up, so go and see for yourself whether your school's government-subsidized menus pass the taste, sight, and smell test.

If the British can revolutionize school food, why can't we do it in North America? The answer was writ large in Oregon in 2005 when a bill introduced in the state legislature that would ban schools from selling soft drinks, candy, and doughnuts and replace them with milk, water, and juice fizzled.

Those fighting over the bill included lobbyists, who said good eating habits should be taught at home and not in schools; school food service directors, who said that getting rid of these profitable items would break school budgets; and school boards and administrators, who said they'd rather hire more physical education teachers than get rid of profitable vending machines that sell junk foods. Contracts with beverage and snack companies can bring in tens of thousands of dollars to school districts starved for cash, and switching to healthier snacks would mean smaller profits for schools. This is what we are teaching our children about our values—money talks, no matter who it hurts.

According to recent government studies and the consensus of nutrition experts several things have become evident:

- Nationwide, three out of four schools serve too much fat
- Too many schools undercut their healthy offerings by placing junk-food filled vending machines just outside the lunchroom
- Schools never have enough vegetables and fruits
- Too little has been done to teach good eating habits

However, there are a few bright signs. A growing number of remarkable, innovative programs are teaching children about food and nutrition and offering them healthier, more delicious meals at school. They are models of what can be accomplished if you demand more for your kids.

Campaigns for Healthy Schools

Alice Waters, the doyenne of new American cuisine and the founder of the Edible Schoolyard Project, believes that how we feed ourselves is as important as all other activities of mankind. She asks, how can we submit so unthinkingly to the dehumanizing experience of lifeless fast food? She asks, "How can you marvel at the world and then feed yourself in such an un-marvelous way?" Waters believes it's because we don't learn the vital relationship of food to culture and agriculture and how food affects the quality of our lives every day.

When we understand where our food comes from, we look at the world in an entirely different manner. Food is not only the source of our spiritual inspiration but also of our physical nourishment. Children should learn that taking care of the land and feeding ourselves are every bit as important as reading, writing, and arithmetic. Our families are not teaching this, so it's up to the schools to teach kids these important values. There should be a garden in every school, and the school lunch program should serve the things children grow themselves, supplemented by local, organically grown products, says Waters. And that is exactly what Alice Waters has accomplished at the Martin Luther King, Jr., Middle School in Berkeley, California.

A Delicious Revolution

Ten years ago, the King school in Berkeley was the local public school for a diverse group of one thousand sixth, seventh, and eighth graders whose parents spoke over twenty languages. The school cafeteria had been closed because it couldn't accommodate that number of students. Instead, prepackaged, microwaved foods were sold to students from a shack at the end of the school parking lot. The schoolyard had been blacktopped, but it was large and members of the community realized that it was the right size for an enormous garden.

Soon a plan took shape to transform the blacktop yard into an "edible landscape" where students would plant and take care of a garden and learn to cook, serve, and eat together in a renovated cafeteria lunchroom. And that's what they did, with the help of a visionary principal.

Today, the Edible Schoolyard is a one-acre organic garden and a kitchen-classroom. Students are involved in all aspects of planting, cultivating, preparing, serving, and eating their food. At lunch, kids sit around picnic tables in the schoolyard, eating salads full of vegetables they've grown themselves, treating each other politely. Troubled kids who've been given a second chance work in the garden and become so transformed by the experience that they come back to act as mentors to new students.

It's not entirely a new idea. Montessori and Waldorf schools, among others, practice similar types of experiential learning. At the King school, learning is a pleasure and kids do so *and* have fun outside of the classroom. They learn with all their senses while picking berries or making curry with twenty-seven aromatic spices. Alice Waters says, "Twenty percent of the U.S. population is in school. Imagine if all these students were preparing food and eating lunch together, our entire agriculture would change overnight, along with our food culture. People would grow up knowing how to cook affordable, wholesome, and delicious food."

Waters is calling for a delicious revolution in our schools to breathe new life and dignity into learning how to eat and to halt the shocking child obesity epidemic that continues to escalate. For more about the Edible Schoolyard and how to implement it in your school, go to the website www.ecoliteracy.org.

Healthy, Organic Lunches in the Heartland

The Royal Cuisine food service of the Hopkins School District in Minnesota serves pizza on whole-wheat crust, sandwiches on whole-grain bread, organic milk, and two fruits and six raw or lightly cooked fresh vegetables along with an extensive salad bar daily. Feeding nine thousand students in kindergarten through twelfth grade, the program is drawing national attention. Students report feeling better after eating these lunches compared to the high-carb, high-fat, high-salt meals they used to eat.

Three-quarters of the offerings are made from scratch on the premises and relatively few brand-name foods are used. French fries are a choice, but portions are down-sized. Sweet foods are made with sugar, not high fructose corn syrup, and locally grown foods are used whenever possible. The district's food is so popular that the school food service provides the catering for local athletic events and banquets and sells take-home meals in the evening.

Action for Healthy Kids

Action for Healthy Kids is a grassroots program guided by a coalition of forty national organizations and government agencies concerned with health, physical activity, and children's eating behavior and activity patterns. Led by a former surgeon general of the United States, Dr. David

Satcher, and chaired by First Lady Laura Bush, teams have been organized in all fifty states and the District of Columbia to carry out action plans to improve school meals and teach nutrition in the classroom. It's too early to tell how much these modestly funded efforts, begun in 2002, will accomplish, but some programs seem to be off to a good start:

- **The CookShop Program of NYC.** This program uses hands-on cooking to promote awareness of and experience with fruits, vegetables, and whole grains in New York City's low-income communities. Classroom learning ties in with the foods served in the school lunch program. Teams of parents and university students work with teachers to bring food experiences into reading, writing, science, and social studies curricula. The emphasis is on fresh, minimally processed fruits, vegetables, and grains. Local sponsors are the New York City Board of Education, NYC Community School Districts 1, 3, and 4, and New York, Columbia, and City Universities. Funding is from the U.S. Department of Agriculture, Health and Human Services, and private funders.

- **Food on the Run.** Organized by California Project Lean, Food on the Run helps low-income California communities design healthy eating and physical activity messages and policies for high schools. Emphasis is placed on creating environments that promote healthy eating and physical activity among teens. Student advocates are trained to conduct activities in high schools, and results are evaluated for effectiveness within school districts. Sponsors are the Public Health Institute and the California Department of

Health Services. Funding comes from the California Endowment, Centers for Disease Control (CDC), U.S. Department of Agriculture, and the California Cancer Research Program.

- **Michigan's Food for Thought.** This project is a cross-curricular outreach program for children from prekindergarten to third grade that links nutrition and reading. Components include a take-home nutrition book bag for parents, families, and students, nutrition theme weeks coordinated with the Reading Is Fundamental program, and in-school activities for children, teachers, and parents. A similar program linking reading with physical activity is underway as a result of the success of the nutrition program.

These are wonderful programs implemented by dedicated people who know why it's important for children to learn about healthy eating. Our students are flunking healthy eating, and their failure is our future. Only 2 percent of schoolchildren meet all of the food pyramid recommendations for healthy eating. Sixteen percent do not meet any of the recommendations. Yet we know that even mild undernutrition can have a lasting impact on children's learning ability, mental health, and thought processes. Even just skipping breakfast alone will adversely affect children's problem-solving abilities.

Appetite for Change: A Campaign for Healthy Schools

Appetite for Change is a nationwide campaign of the Organic Consumers Association to make school food programs healthy and sustainable, integrate organic foods and nontoxic products into school meals programs, and create a safer and healthier environment for children to learn in. The campaign has four goals:

- Stop the spraying of toxic pesticides on school grounds and buildings
- Kick junk foods and junk food ads out of schools
- Convert school meals into healthier menus using organic ingredients and offering vegetarian options
- Teach students about healthy food choices through school garden projects and classroom curricula

At the Appetite for Change website (www.organic consumers.org/sos.htm), you can download materials and resources that can be used in your local schools. You also can find out how you can be part of an Appetite for Change network in your own area.

What Else Can We Do?

Obesity isn't a small problem, and small fixes won't make the problem go away. The problem is continuing to get worse, and small solutions aren't likely to make a dent in children's deteriorating health and nutrition situation. For one thing, no one's fully in charge. Our schools are struggling to be the solution, but they have a lot on their plates because they're expected to do so much with so little. Always short of cash, schools can't get the supplies and special programs they need (band, computers, sports uniforms) unless they have additional resources from the community. Over the years, soft drink, snack food, and kid-TV companies have been the main sources of support for many communities. This needs to change.

Government brochures about nutrition, food-related issues, and guidelines are sensitive to every interest group's concerns. The food industry has the most to gain and lose in this situation, and it plies its interests seamlessly, seducing kids with "loot," action heroes, cool ads, and Web games. Why can't we get junk food out of our schools? Why can't national nutritional improvement get as much of our attention as a space launch or fighting terrorists? The answer lies in the short attention spans of our government officials, the media, and ourselves. The United States is missing the boat and falling behind the rest of the industrialized world.

Other industrialized countries are taking the threat of a generation maimed by poor diet seriously. In 2005, the Irish government banned television advertising for fast foods and candy. British health authorities are threatening to ban junk food advertising unless marketers take useful actions on their own. The European Health Commissioner gave the food industry one year to stop advertising to children entirely and threatens legislation if results are not seen.

It used to be considered a peculiarly American problem, but childhood obesity has increased steadily in Europe over the past twenty years as American fast foods, soft drinks, and snacks have gone global. Close to one in five European children now are overweight. But in Europe, unlike North America, governments are standing up to the food industry.

What Do Kids Want?

What do kids really want? A contest by the Center for a New American Dream asked kids that question. Their answers were surprising. The most common answers were "love," "happiness," "peace on earth," and "friends." Significant numbers of children also wanted time with family, a clean environment, a world where people treat each other with respect, a chance to see lost loved ones, help for suffering people, good health, and time to play.

But what children do has less to do with what they want and more to do with what they learn from the media. According to a study by the Kaiser Family Foundation released in March 2005, children and teens are spending increasing amounts of time connected with media—using computers, playing video games, watching TV, and listening to music.

Most kids have TVs and DVD players in their bedrooms, and many also have computers, cable TV, Internet access, fax machines, and stereos. Most report that they have been given no rules for watching TV by their parents and that the TV usually is on during mealtimes, even when no one is watching. In other words, kids are living in an increasingly message-driven environment with relatively few of the messages coming from their parents.

When we abdicate mealtimes to the TV we are abandoning our children to exploitation by commercial interests whose only objective is to manipulate them into becoming überconsumers. Isn't it time you rethought mealtimes? Make breakfast, lunch, and dinner a special time for family connection and enjoying the pleasures of eating good food together. Chapter 4 provides ideas and a plan for doing that.

Healthy Eating 101

There is a wisdom in the body beyond the rules of physic. A man's own observations, what he finds good of and hurt of, is the best physic to preserve health.

—Sir Francis Bacon

Although you've chalked it up to getting older, you've lost some of the oomph you once had and you feel run down and tired a lot of the time. You have a vague sense that you're not operating on all of your cylinders, but you're not sure whether to blame it on work and stress on the job, family pressures, or something not quite right in your body. Thinking about it makes you shudder; you have willed yourself not to be sick—you can't afford the time or money! You try not to think about it, which makes you think about it all the more.

You'd like to lose weight, tone up, and find an elixir of youth, but even if you sign up for weight loss classes and yoga, you know that you won't have the patience to keep it up for long, and eventually you'll feel even more disappointed and depressed when you're right back where you started. As to the elixir of youth, your physician laughs when you mention it, saying you are in good shape for your age and suggesting a vacation, a spa treatment, or a cosmetic makeover. You leave the office feeling misunderstood and rejected by the medical establishment, and you vow never to reveal your personal struggles to your doctor again.

You are left with a nagging sense that there is something you can do that will give you back your edge. Should you trust this impression or get over it and move on? Sit with the feeling for a moment and try to get a better sense of just what your gut is trying to tell you. Did you know that your gut is your second brain? It may not say anything in words the way your rational mind does, but it does react to things you are about to do that may not be so good for you. When something doesn't sit well with us, it probably isn't right and is best avoided. But realize that unless you take the time to calm down and wait for the impression from your gut to surface, your rational mind probably will override your gut and urge you to revert to the old ways that have been your habit until now.

Your mind knows what you have been doing and likes you to stay on track, while your gut wants to steer you away from danger. It's what protected our ancient ancestors from wild animals and dangerous environments. Animals and so-called primitive people sense danger better than we do. Did you read about the tribe in Indonesia that sensed the coming of the great tsunami of 2004, moving up into the hills and away from danger before the big waves came and swept everything away? They relied on their well-developed instinct for sensing danger to guide them to safety. Would you have trusted your gut in that situation?

Dr. Judith Petry, M.D., F.A.C.S., a former reconstructive surgeon and now the medical director of the Vermont Healing Tools Project, says, "Our bodies do have voices. They are most often drowned out by the constant babble of the world we create for ourselves, but they are there, waiting, and willing to tell us what they need. Most often subtle and quiet, the voices get louder as we refuse to listen."

Have you ever been invited to a big, fancy dinner by a friend, and your reaction was to feel physically ill at the prospect of the very rich meal? Dr. Petry says it's your gut objecting to the meal. In that circumstance, you have a choice. You can avoid the meal that your gut doesn't want—one that might make you ill if you ate it, or you can join your friend in the meal, ignoring your body's warnings and taking one of the little purple pills advertised for indigestion. Many of us have done that for far too long. That is why so many of us (70 million by a recent government count) suffer from indigestion, GERD (gastroesophageal reflux disease), and irritable bowel disease. (See Chapter 8 for information on healing digestive disorders.)

Harmful behaviors like smoking and eating the wrong foods are the hardest to avoid, says Dr. Petry, because the slow, long-term harm they cause isn't apparent to us. But we can learn to hear the inner voice of caution and avoid what otherwise might slowly kill or maim us. When we listen to that voice we connect with an ancient part of our biology, an emotional intelligence neglected and ridiculed by Western medicine, for which we pay dearly both in physical and emotional terms.

The Problem with the Pyramid

The USDA's new Food Pyramid Guide was presented to the public in 2005 in a colorful graphic of a pyramid made up of five converging colorful stripes representing the five food groups, with a stick figure of a person climbing stairs at the side. (See Figure 4.1.) The graphic was accompanied by a website where you can enter your personal profile and obtain one of twelve pyramids matched to your estimated calorie needs, specifying how many servings of five food groups—grains, vegetables, fruits, milk, meat and beans—you should eat daily. You can see the pyramid and find the right pyramid for you at www.mypyramid.gov.

The USDA's new food guidance system, as it is called, is built around calories as the central nutrition factor for determining your ideal diet. Considering the explosion of fatness in North America over the last three decades, the USDA's central focus on calories means that all foods have a place at your table, even those we commonly think of as junk foods, as long as you have room for spare calories. In trying to please everybody, makers of junk foods as well as nutritionally important foods, the USDA has repeated the nutrition fallacy that has been its theme for seventy years, "All foods are good foods," a theme that has gotten us into trouble and is nutritionally unsupported.

Research over the last ten years has shown the types of foods, ingredients, and eating patterns that are beneficial for health and weight, yet these factors are given little or no attention in the new guide. In the first food pyramid, the stacked, horizontal bars representing food groups indicated that some foods—those at the tip of the pyramid—should be eaten less often because they are less valuable nutritionally.

Figure 4.1 New Food Pyramid Graphic—www.MyPyramid.gov

The new graphic shifts the emphasis away from best food choices to a new food democracy where every food is equal. It is provoking many questions. More than half of all consumers in a nationwide survey responded that they were confused and unclear about how to follow the new pyramid.

Leaving aside the feasibility of 270 million people being able to access the USDA's special website, which on the first day of the new guide's release could not be seen by the two to three million people trying to access it, how will people know where to get more information? An advertising expert I consulted, who played a leading role in creating the new USDA food guide, told me it would cost a minimum of $300 million a year to promote the new guide effectively. No USDA funds were earmarked for this purpose.

But the USDA has a plan. It is relying on the food industry to market the new guide. As one grocery association official put it, the USDA is "passing the baton to the food industry to help educate Americans to make small changes to meet the [dietary] guidelines." But, isn't that what got us into trouble to begin with?

Losing no time, the Idaho Potato Commission announced that it believes the new USDA food guidance system will help set the record straight about carbohydrates, including potatoes, which they claim are the best fuel for muscles. "Our biggest job right now is to tell the nutritional story about Idaho potatoes. We understand that America is waging a fierce weight battle, but there is no logical reason to target food products that are so naturally good for you. It's that simple," says Frank Muir, president of the Potato Commission. And maybe the new food guidance system is that simple. We shouldn't expect it to be a tool for health promotion based on the latest scientific studies about healthy eating. That's not what it was designed for.

People have a lot of questions about nutrition and are told different things at every turn by physicians, teachers, dietitians, the government, and food marketers. Isn't it time the questions were answered directly by knowledgeable, independent authorities without a vested interest? Calories are not the only things that count. You also need to know which foods are critical to good health and which ones undermine it. The "Ten Rules for Healthy Eating" in Chapter 2 and my Guide to Healthy Eating in this chapter are intended to help meet that need.

Guide to Healthy Eating

The Guide to Healthy Eating shown in Figure 4.2 is a newer, healthier alternative to the USDA's food pyramid guide. It resembles the USDA's guide in shape but not in content because it is built exclusively of foods and portions that are best choices for a healthful diet. It doesn't include nutritionally deficient foods because they should be treated as occasional rather than everyday choices. This guide is a result of my work in nutrition and it makes no attempt to embrace everything sold in the supermarket. Instead, it prioritizes foods on the basis of their nutrient density, favorable ratios of nutrients, and antioxidants to calories.

My food guide's emphasis is on foods that come from growing plants: vegetables, fruits, grains, beans, nuts, and

Figure 4.2 The author's alternative food pyramid: The Guide to Healthy Eating

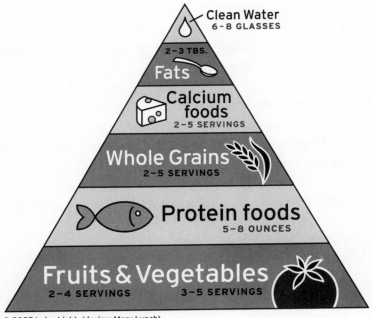

Clean Water
6-8 GLASSES

2-3 TBS.
Fats

Calcium foods
2-5 SERVINGS

Whole Grains
2-5 SERVINGS

Protein foods
5-8 OUNCES

Fruits & Vegetables
2-4 SERVINGS   3-5 SERVINGS

© 2005 Luise Light (design: Mary Lynch)

seed/nut oils, but it is designed to please meat and dairy eaters as well as vegetarians. Like all traditional food guides, it is a way to convert what nutritionists know about foods, nutrition, and health into a practical plan for food selection. The Guide to Healthy Eating was developed with these goals in mind:

- Meeting the nutritional needs of people with different ethnic food backgrounds
- Helping people choose diets that meet the nutrient levels recommended by national and international health and nutrition authorities
- Highlighting foods that are sources of "problem" nutrients that are short in many diets
- Including a variety of foods that are readily available and nutritionally valuable
- Increasing awareness of traditional foods that are important sources of nutrients used by people with diverse culinary traditions

In order to decide whether a particular food is a good choice for you, consider the various ingredients in the food. Here are some questions for you to consider about pizza, for example:

- Is there enough tomato sauce to count as a serving of vegetable?
- Is the crust whole grain?
- Is the cheese natural or processed?
- What kind of oil was used, is it good or bad fat?
- If meats are used, what kinds of meats are they and what additives are in them?

That may seem like a lot to consider for one or two slices of mouth-watering pizza. They are not the kinds of questions you want to think about when you're standing at the counter ordering your pie. But if pizza is one of your favorites, you might want to do some research online or at the library to find answers to assist you in later food decisions. Consider your choices before you come face-to-face with them. Eating a favorite food like pizza occasionally may not be a problem, but a steady diet of it is something else.

Your Personal Diet Makeover

We know that food is critical to health. It also is crucial to survival from deadly diseases. Recent studies have shown that dietary factors such as having enough vitamin D and eating red chili peppers and cruciferous vegetables such as broccoli are important to surviving lung, pancreatic, and ovarian cancers. So what should we do? Become vegetarians, eat only rabbit food? You don't have to go to that extreme. In fact, it's really very simple. Start by finding out how your daily diet stacks up. You may be surprised at what you find out.

Your Daily Diet Reality Check

"I don't really eat that much—why am I gaining so much weight?" a friend of mine asked me. He claimed to be eating much less meat, bread, and sweets than in years past, yet his weight was ballooning. "There's only one way to know what's going on," I told him, "Look your diet squarely in the eye and find out." At that point, I pulled out a copy of my healthy eating checklist and handed it to him. He's yet to return it to me, but many others have and have found it an eye-opener.

If you want to weigh in on whether your diet needs an overhaul, here's a quick and easy way to do it without tallying up all those grams, milligrams, and ounces. It won't tell you the exact levels of nutrients you are eating, but it will show where your eating is weak or unbalanced, and it will give you a target to aim at for improvement.

Based on the Guide to Healthy Eating in Figure 4.2 and the "Ten Rules for Healthy Eating," discussed in Chapter 2, this list allows you to evaluate your daily diet in terms of two critical criteria: your healthy eating score, which represents how your eating compares to the recommended number of servings in the Guide to Healthy Eating; and your food risk score, which is the number of commercial foods you're eating that contain ingredients known to promote weight gain or raise your risks for major chronic diseases. These include foods and drinks made with commercial sweeteners, artificial sweeteners, and white flour, are deep-fried, or contain MSG/glutamates. Here's how to do it:

- Add the number of servings you consumed that day from each of the five food groups and total it (water should not be included in this tally).
- Compare your total to the total number of recommended daily servings (16 for women and 30 for men).

- Next, subtract 2 points from your score for every food group that is not represented in your day's diet. For example, if you're a woman and your score was 11 but you didn't eat any fruits and vegetables that day, you would subtract 2 points from your total for a final tally of 9.

Your healthy eating score would be: $9/16 \times 100 = 56$ percent.

To obtain your food risk score, add the number of servings of food and drinks you consumed that were pre-sweetened, artificially sweetened, made with white flour, deep- or batter fried, and contained MSG or glutamate (a flavor enhancer).

Add your number of food risk factors to your recommended number of servings. For example, you found 4 food risk factors (2 soft drinks, 1 bag of potato chips, and 1 bagel). You would add 4 to 16 if you are a woman or 4 to 30 if you are a man. If your healthy eating score is 56 percent and your food risk factors are also 50 percent, that might be confusing and overwhelming. If the latter was 25 percent, it automatically gives you hope for improvement that is realistic.

Your food risk score would be $4/20 \times 100$, or 25 percent for a woman, and $4/34 \times 100$, or 12 percent for a man.

Use these scores as targets for improvement.

Foods Are Not Simple

Food groupings are a traditional way of classifying foods on the basis of similar nutritional content. This approach works better when popular foods and eating patterns favor fresh, minimally processed, traditional foods and recipes. But today, most foods eaten in the Western world are stripped down and reassembled foods and combinations of ingredients prepared by fast-food chains and processed food companies. Because you don't know what's gone into them, it's not easy to know where these foods fit in the food pyramid.

Foods often contain two or more major ingredients that belong in more than one food group category. For example, for macaroni and cheese you'd score 1 for a calcium food, 1 for protein (cheese), and 1 risk factor for a white flour food (macaroni). Pizza counts as 1 white flour food (crust), 1 vegetable (tomato sauce and peppers), 1 calcium food (cheese), and 1 protein food (cheese, meat). Remember, we're not trying to do a scientific analysis here, just a quick-and-dirty look at how well your diet rates in terms of healthfulness.

To get a better idea of how to calculate your scores, I've included the diet checklist of a young man who came to me for nutrition advice. Josh was twenty-five years old, five feet, five inches tall, and weighed 275 pounds. He was under treatment by his physician for psoriasis and an underactive thyroid. He knew his eating needed an extreme makeover, but he didn't know where or how to start. Here is the three-day food diary Josh handed to me when we met:

Wednesday

Chicken salad wrap with light mayo
20 ounces Pepsi

½ cup ice cream (Ben & Jerry's)
2 grilled cheese sandwiches
Glass of milk
12-ounce can Fresca
Altoids

Thursday

2 8-ounce glasses pink lemonade
Bagel with cream cheese
Iced coffee with milk and sugar
Chicken rice soup
Shrimp with fried rice
2 wantons
20 ounces Fresca
2 pieces of toast
2 light beers
Peanut butter and jelly sandwich
Glass of milk

Friday

2 pieces of toast
Mug of coffee with milk and sugar
12-ounce can Fresca
2 chocolate chip cookies
2 8-ounce glasses pink lemonade
20 ounces Fresca
Baked macaroni and cheese
Bread and butter
Salad
12-ounce can Fresca

Here are Josh's healthy eating and food risk scores, based on his diet diary:

Josh's Healthy Eating Score

	DAY 1	DAY 2	DAY 3
Fruits and vegetables (5 to 9 servings)	0	0	1
Protein foods (5 to 8 ounces)	1	3	1
Whole grains (2 to 5 servings)	0	0	0
Calcium foods (2 to 5 servings)	4	1	1
Fats (2 to 3 tablespoons)	1	2	2
Healthy Eating Scores	**6.5%**	**6.5%**	**10%**

Food Risk Score

	DAY 1	DAY 2	DAY 3
Sweetened foods and drinks	2	4	2
Artificially sweetened drinks	1	1	3
White flour foods	5	4	5
Fried foods	0	2	0
MSG foods	2	4	2
Risk Factor Scores	**25%**	**33%**	**29%**

Josh's current diet was poor in nutrients and antioxidants and very high in sugars and white flour foods, a high glycemic index diet that, along with obesity, makes him prone to type 2 diabetes. Josh ate no fresh fruit or (with one exception) vegetables, which meant his diet was low or deficient in many vitamins and minerals, making him prone to inflammatory conditions such as the psoriasis and arthritis, from which he suffered. The absence of any fiber-rich foods in his diet (whole grains, vegetables, and fruits) raised his risks for heart disease and several types of cancer. Also, Josh had no obvious source of good fats such as omega-3 fatty acids to counteract the formation of proinflammatory factors.

I recommended to Josh an anti-inflammatory diet rich in antioxidant fruits and vegetables, whole grains, wild fish, organic poultry, eggs, dairy foods, olive oil, and other monounsaturated and omega-3 fats; moderate exercise for a half hour daily; stress management; avoiding alcohol, spicy foods, shellfish, red meats (except pasture-fed animals); and plenty of sleep. We worked out a program that allowed him to make these changes over a five-week period.

This worked for Josh, but you may require other changes. The important thing is not to make all of the changes at once and to realize that the changes take time to get used to. This program was not easy for Josh, who knew very little about food and nutrition when we started working together. But his weight loss progress, better energy levels, and decreased pain from arthritis reinforced his commitment to continue the program. His weight loss is slow and he would like to see faster results, but he realizes that he is making progress and he feels much better and more optimistic.

Changing Without Tears

Change is hard for everyone. But knowing what to do to dissipate the discomfort it causes helps. For example, you may try giving up sweets, but sweets may not give you up so fast or easily. When you crave sweets, instead of reaching for a sweet snack, eat a small amount of protein foods such as nuts or a slice of turkey breast. It will calm your craving. After a few days, the craving will seem to disappear. It really doesn't go away, however, just underground. If you allow yourself to binge on sweets at a later time, you will become a sugar junkie once again and have to go through the struggle of giving it up once more.

Your body will adapt to your new eating style in time, and the longer you follow it the better you'll feel. You know from what you've read in earlier chapters that there is a problem with the synthetic, overprocessed, industrially engineered foods filling our supermarkets and that most of us overeat on foods limited in or devoid of the natural nutrition we need to nourish and regulate our body's cells. Also, packaged foods and packaging itself contain toxic chemicals that leach into our bodies creating disease. A well-nourished body has the ability to resist disease and heal itself, but when an immune system is weakened by toxicity and poor nutrition these abilities are compromised. Medications can help you tolerate the burden of disease, but they don't help you release what is causing you to feel ill or exhausted.

You may be wondering, "What foods should I eat for greater energy and a more upbeat feeling?" Try this simple experiment. Set out four small plates: one with slices of fresh, colorful fruit, one with pieces of fresh, colorful vegetables, and two with chips and candy. Add to these a glass of cola and a glass of filtered water. Now, sitting calmly, place your hand over each dish and glass, in turn. Write down what your gut tells you; which foods and drinks seem to have the best energy? Which ones seem the most lifeless? Trust what you "hear." The answers usually are readily apparent.

Keep a Journal

The first thing I advise people to do who come to me for help with nutrition problems is to keep a journal for three days marking down everything they put in their mouths. I instruct them to be specific with the names of the foods and drinks they consume, the times they consume them, and the amounts. Many people object, saying they don't have the time or aren't good at keeping track of things. However, this is a critical step in determining what's going on nutritionally and coming to grips with their emotional eating patterns and the quantities and types of foods they are eating that they may not be aware of.

Usually, their willingness to come face-to-face with their eating patterns is what determines how successful they will be at making necessary changes in their eating. If they can't look at their behavior and learn how they are setting themselves up for difficulties, they probably have not yet reached the point where they want to make health-promoting changes. It means they either don't have the confidence that they can feel better or they are afraid to let go of the lifeboat of what their doctors tell them: "Don't worry about your diet, we have a pill for that."

Most of the time, most of us stuff food down barely aware we are eating. We eat while multitasking, reading the paper or a report from the office, or while watching

TV. Eating in our culture has become a semiconscious, throwaway behavior except for those special occasions when we celebrate holidays and events with the family. As a result of our perfunctory eating, we don't chew our food well or pay attention to the inner signals that tell us that what we are eating or drinking is going to cause us distress. Eating too much rich, greasy foods and drinking too many bubbly soft drinks—the types of meals we shovel down in fast-food restaurants and pizza parlors—can lead to GERD and other GI problems. When you experience indigestion, you probably have to cut down on eating until the pain subsides.

Women concerned about their weight often cut down to the point where they are not eating enough calories. But if you don't consume enough calories you are sabotaging yourself by slowing down your metabolism and making weight loss even harder, if not impossible. Eating enough calories keeps your metabolism working more efficiently, which makes weight loss a lot easier. This probably sounds counterintuitive to you because all of your life you've heard that calories count! They do, but not when you drop below 1,100 calories daily and you've gone through years of yo-yo dieting. Eating too few calories brings in your body's internal equivalent of "homeland security," protecting you from what your body reads as the danger of starvation. When that happens, the motto "calories count" takes on a whole new meaning—your body will conserve all the calories it can by storing them as fat.

A journal will not only show you how little you are eating, but also whether you are shorting yourself on essential nutrients. If you don't eat the suggested minimum number of daily food servings illustrated in Figure 4.2, you could come up short on some important nutrients— and provide another excuse for your essential cell functions to slow down.

You may experience this slowdown as a lack of energy, feelings of depletion, sadness, anxiety, or pessimism, or minor aches, numbness, or pain. These symptoms of subclinical malnutrition tend to be generalized and nonspecific. Too vague to be pinned down clinically, they are often chalked up to a patient's imagination or the need for more of a physician's attention. But that's incorrect. There are just so many ways your body can express not feeling up to par. The symptoms are real and affect your functional health, even if modern medicine can't label what is wrong. Your symptoms should alert you to take a long, hard look at what you're eating and drinking.

When you review your journal, put a check next to the foods you want to avoid or exchange for healthier types. Consider what you might substitute for the foods and eating occasions you've targeted for improvement. Which whole grains will you exchange for bakery products made with refined white flour? Which foods and drinks sweetened with natural sweeteners (honey, maple syrup, fruit purees) or unsweetened will you use to replace the presweetened foods and drinks you buy from the convenience store or the vending machine? You'll need much smaller amounts of natural sweeteners to sweeten foods yourself compared to the amounts typically added to foods and drinks by manufacturers.

Which fresh, organic, minimally processed foods will you substitute for chemicalized, packaged ones? You will probably consume much less salt, unhealthy fats, and synthetic additives by switching to fresh, whole, organic foods in the amounts suggested in the Guide to Healthy Eating.

Decide in what order you will make your changes. Start with the ones you consider easiest for you; for example, increasing the amount of fruit you eat daily. What time of day will you eat fruit? Here are a few ideas. Take an apple or pear to work as a midmorning snack, and select a wedge of melon or some grapes as an after-dinner sweet instead of a dessert. If your target is to eat three servings of fruit a day, you could add a small bowl of berries topped with unsweetened yogurt (with some maple syrup or a few chocolate chips, if you like it sweet) as a midafternoon snack, or nibble on a small handful of raisins and nuts on the way home from work. There are a lot of ways to increase fruit; two that I was treated to recently were appetizers of Medjool dates stuffed with a soft, creamy white cheese, and slices of fresh pear and apple served with a honeyed chili pepper–yogurt dip.

Make a plan for adding vegetables. Any eating occasion is the right occasion for sneaking more vegetables into your diet. For example, if you order a turkey wrap at lunch, tell the kitchen staff to stuff it with as many vegetables as possible. If you make (or order) an omelet, load it up with veggies. A big lunch salad from the salad bar with beans, greens, red peppers, red cabbage, and so on can count for two servings of veggies. Or try a hummus sandwich on multigrain sourdough bread for lunch.

Add a dinner appetizer of baba ghanoush, made of roasted eggplant, lemon, garlic, and sesame seed paste and accompanied by wedges of whole-wheat pita bread and raw veggies for dipping. Heap vividly colored vegetables on your dinner plate, and you won't find it hard to hit your mark. But a word of caution: make the vegetable and whole-grain changes slowly, over several days and weeks, or you may find yourself feeling uncomfortably bloated. Vegetables are high in natural fiber. They are beneficial for your health, but your GI tract needs time to adjust to this bulkier, more fibrous food. Write down a plan to make eating changes in daily and weekly increments. Carry a copy of your plan with you for quick reference when shopping or eating out.

As you add whole foods in exchange for juices and packaged foods, you may feel as if you are eating too much food. The reason you feel this is because the processed foods you are used to eating are more concentrated in calories and much lower in fiber than whole, unprocessed foods. That is why you can eat so much more of those foods without negative feedback from your gut. Processed foods are partially "digested" chemically before they reach you, so you can eat a lot more of them without feeling too full or uncomfortable. But here's the kicker: they also are absorbed more quickly so you get more calories per ounce before your body has a chance to say stop, enough! Also, synthetic flavorings trick your palate into believing you have eaten something that not only tastes good but also is good for you. You end up eating more because your body, which can't be fooled, keeps looking for the real nutrition it needs and continues to make you want to eat more food.

Unless you plan how you are going to make eating changes, you are likely to revert to your old ways of eating automatically. In order to break your old habits, you have to make change a conscious priority. Experts say that it can take twenty-one days to break a habit, so you need to be patient with yourself. Glance at a copy of your plan for daily changes before you start meal preparations. If you prepare food for others as well as yourself, tell them what you are planning to do and ask for their cooperation. If they say they don't like veggies or want bigger portions of meat, or they don't want to give up desserts, you may have to vary their menus and add some of their favorites to your plan.

Men and teenage boys need more calories than women and girls, so they require bigger servings, and a few extras won't hurt them. But even if they say they don't like vegetables, they are likely to be surprised at how good organic produce tastes, and how good they feel after a healthy meal. Even your friend, partner, or spouse can shift to healthier tastes if you gradually introduce changes to the meals you share. Focus on the healthy foods your significant others already like, like salad, dipping vegetables, or blenderized fruit yogurt drinks.

How Foods Affect You

Your genetic inheritance plays an important role in how foods affect you. If you come from a family where the risk of diabetes and heart disease is high, you need to select more low glycemic index foods (foods that slowly convert to glucose) and fewer high glycemic ones, as well as less commercial meats and more fish and fowl.

Whole grains and beans are digested and enter the body more slowly so they have less of an impact on insulin secretion, which responds to the amount of sugars released from the starches and sweets you've eaten. Less insulin means a lower glycemic load and lower risk of diabetes. The more insulin you secrete the more likely it is that your body's insulin will lose its effectiveness. Harvard researchers have found that the risk of diabetes is two and a half times greater for women who eat the most sugar and refined starches such as white bread, pasta, and potatoes. In general, whole foods tend to be lower glycemic and processed foods higher glycemic.

- **Low glycemic foods.** Black beans, broccoli, cherries, leafy vegetables, milk, peanuts, peanut butter, pears, plums, soybeans, tomatoes, wild rice, yogurt
- **Moderately low glycemic foods.** All-Bran, apples, garbanzo beans (chickpeas), ice cream, navy beans, oranges, peas, pinto beans, potato chips
- **Moderately high glycemic foods.** Bananas, candy bars, potatoes, white pita bread, oat bran, oat bread, raisins, carrots, brown rice, kidney beans
- **High glycemic foods.** Bagels, basmati rice, cakes, Cheerios, corn, corn flakes, pies, pretzels, pasta, white bread

If you are carbohydrate-sensitive and also need to avoid refined grains, try not to consume too much whole wheat, rye, oats, or millet. You need some grains in your diet for their B vitamins and important minerals, but you may want to try modest amounts of spelt, quinoa, brown rice, buckwheat groats, whole-grain bulgur, amaranth, and beans as well. Also, when grains are soaked and/or fermented through a sourdough process, you may find you can digest them better. When preparing oatmeal, for example, soak the oats overnight and add a tablespoon of yogurt (with a live culture) to facilitate fermentation. You might also try genuine sourdough bread, which many people with grain intolerances find less troublesome.

Be alert for products labeled whole grain, like many commercial breakfast cereals, breads, and bagels, that contain only a small amount of whole grains. Read the ingredient labels. Unbleached wheat flour, cornmeal, and pearled barley are not whole grains. A good rule of thumb is to avoid foods that say "enriched" on the label. It means that some nutrients have been added back because the real nutrients were stripped out in processing. There is also some evidence that the synthetic nutrients added back may be harmful to your liver. It can be very confusing. Don't be fooled.

If you are from a family where the risk of cancer is high, you might want to adopt this recommendation of the American Institute for Cancer Research for protection against common cancers: fill two-thirds of your plate with a variety of plant foods such as fruits, vegetables, whole grains, and beans, and one-third or less with animal proteins. Most of us have been doing it in reverse for a long time.

Whatever your health risks, don't avoid healthy fats (see the description of healthy fats in Chapter 2), especially omega-3 fatty acids. They are needed in every cell of your body, especially by your nervous system. Our modern diets are naturally low in healthy fats, so we often have to rely on supplements. Look for the best quality fish oil or flaxseed oil supplements for your daily omega-3 fatty acids. Other healthy fats include natural, minimally processed, or organic olive oil, butter, organic coconut oil, avocados, nuts (especially walnuts, almonds, and peanuts), and seeds of all kinds.

Weighing in on Weight

Eating the best quality food is one of the easiest ways to create health on a daily basis. Many people compromise their nutrition because they want to lose weight and be thin. Our society continually tells us that we can never be too thin, so we starve ourselves. But undercutting nutrition is one of the most common reasons why people find it hard to lose weight.

When we struggle to avoid almost all natural fats and carbohydrates in favor of high-protein, highly processed, diet-friendly foods, we don't function at our best. We have survived as a species through the ages because we learned to select and digest the natural foods in our environment. When we shift to a synthetic diet of imitation foods that our bodies don't know how to break down, we compromise our digestive processes and, ultimately, our health. Our bodies and our shapes are programmed to change in different ages and stages of life. The challenge is to be both well-nourished and successful at managing weight through each of these ages and stages. You can do it, but it means varying the proportions of fats, carbohydrates, and proteins to get the most efficient ratio of calories. As you go through the various stages of life, you need more high-quality, nutrient-dense calories and fewer calorie-dense fuel foods. See Chapter 9, "Slimming Without

Tears," for more information on how a healthy diet can lead to a slimmer waistline.

In Chapter 5, you'll find a tool kit for putting the Guide to Healthy Eating to work in your life. If you eat the right foods most of the time, the wrong ones infrequently, and exercise moderately, calories take care of themselves.

Your Diet Makeover
Tool Kit

*My kitchen is a mystical place, a kind of temple for me.
It is a place where the surfaces seem to have significance,
where the sounds and odors carry meaning that transfers
from the past and bridges to the future.*

—PEARL BAILEY

Eating well starts in your kitchen. It is where the con-
cept of a balanced diet comes to life in the variety of
foods you keep on hand to stock your cook pots and nourish your health. Whatever else is in your larder may satisfy
your appetite but not your need for nourishment. Review
what's on your pantry shelves. You'll be surprised by the
collection of flavorings, snacks, and cooking ingredients
you've accumulated and forgotten you had. You probably
could go years without needing to replace them.

Instead of getting depressed by what you find, recognize this as an opportunity to reconcile with your "inner nutritionist," the person you are becoming: healed, healthy, younger feeling, and energized. All that stands between you and that ideal may be a pantry makeover, if you are willing to give it a try.

Pantry and Refrigerator Redux

Start by taking all the foods, drinks, and seasonings off your shelves and examining each item in turn to determine whether to place it back on the shelf or not. Make two piles on the counter or the floor, one for the keepers, another for the losers. The keepers remain; the losers have to go.

A pantry makeover has two main purposes:

- Getting rid of the foods and drinks that contain ingredients that can drag down and jeopardize your health
- Making room for foods and drinks whose ingredients can help you achieve optimal health

Cleaning out your pantry and fridge is like shedding old skin after the new skin has begun to grow in; it's painless and liberating. So don't be anxious about losing dear old friends. The only thing dear about recreational products like soda, cookies, and potato chips is their price tags.

Here's what to be on the lookout for in your search for fool's gold: commercial foods, drinks, and ingredients that are greasy, salty, or sweet, made with refined and artificial sugars or industrial fats (hydrogenated, partially hydrogenated, and trans fats), and products made with white flour, including breads, rolls, muffins, rice cakes, crackers, breakfast cereals, pastries, pasta, and taco shells. Also included among the losers are reduced fat (low or no fat) products; smoked meats, fish, and cheese; "fixings" such as flavored nuts, bacon-flavored soy bits for salads, processed cheese (sliced, grated, or extruded); and products containing artificial colors, modified starch, monosodium glutamate (MSG), preservatives, and other additives.

More of the "fun foods" you'll want to junk include instant popcorn; candy and sweets; corn chips; cookies, crackers, and pretzels; instant and quick-cooking grains and cereals; flaked, puffed, and shaped breakfast cereals; salad dressings; breakfast buns and cakes; cake and muffin mixes; instant, canned, and dried soups; canned vegetables; ready-to-eat pasta and stews; commercial sausages and cold cuts; meat jerky and meat-based sticks; protein bars; sandwich spreads; processed dips and sauces; commercial nut butters; commercial vegetable oils; nondairy creamers; commercial (irradiated) herbs and spices; gravies and sauces with glutamate; bouillon powders and cubes, flavoring agents, and meat tenderizers; meat extenders; pickles and relishes; and ketchup. If you're not sure whether an item is a plus or a minus, review the "Ten Rules for Healthy Eating" in Chapter 2 for the details.

Inspect your refrigerator and freezer and clean out products made with damaged (industrial) fats such as french fries, doughnuts, chicken nuggets, fried chicken, or other fast foods—anything made by deep-frying, which, along with processing, turns natural fats into damaged and damaging synthetic oils that the body can't handle. Damaged fats become free radicals that injure cells and cause accelerated aging and chronic disease.

When you see the growing mound of costly losers in your discard pile, you may be thinking, is this pantry holocaust worth it? Yes. This pantry makeover is an act of Home Security. Commercial food products contain substances intentionally added for technological purposes in the manufacture, processing, preparation, treatment, packaging, transport, and storage of food. The most troublesome additives, in terms of the numbers of people who report allergies or sensitivities when they eat them, are:

- Coloring agents. Used to restore color lost in processing
- Preservatives. Such as sulfites, nitrites, and calcium propionate used to extend shelf life
- Taste and texture modifiers. Such as thickeners, emulsifiers, stabilizers, salt, MSG, and sweeteners used to enhance smell, mouth-feel, and taste

In other words, additives fool our palates and sense organs into believing that industrial foods taste, look, and feel like real food.

Some familiar ingredients designed to make faux foods seem real include:

- Hydrolyzed vegetable protein for meat flavor and consistency
- Thickening agents such as carrageenan and guar gum
- The fat substitute Olestra

- Acids and acidity regulators used to control acidity and alkalinity
- Anticaking agents used to keep powders flowing freely
- Antifoaming agents
- Packaging gases used to preserve sliced cooked meats, fish, and seafood

Preservatives also are added to the packages of ready-to-eat raw vegetables and salads found in the chill-cases of your supermarket. Fresh, local food is free of this chemical trickery and lasts longer in your fridge.

Your Makeover Market Basket

We are so used to seeing shopping carts piled high with prepackaged foods that we don't give them a second thought. But when someone wheels a cart brimful of perishables ahead of us in the checkout line we wonder if the person is from a food stamps family. We've been brainwashed into thinking that if food doesn't come in a bag or box, it's probably not as good. But that's the opposite of what's true.

Commercial production, transport, and storage methods have reduced the levels of nutrition in commercial foods. Studies have shown a 30 percent decline in the vitamin and mineral content of commercial fruits and vegetables over the last forty years. Marginal nutrition levels found in large numbers of Americans in recent national nutrition surveys have been attributed to the poor levels of nutrition in conventionally grown foods. There are two types of national nutrition monitoring conducted by the U.S. government. One is a time-trend series of the nutrient evaluations of the U.S. food supply, comparing annual per capita food consumption levels with food guide serving recommendations. This tracking reveals, for example, how many servings of fats, sugars, fruits, vegetables, whole or refined grains, dairy, and meats people are eating, on average, year to year.

The second source of this information is the Continuing National Survey of Food Intakes of Individuals that is part of the National Health and Nutrition Examination Survey conducted jointly by the U.S. Departments of Health and Human Services and the USDA. Researchers from leading medical schools and nutrition departments of universities study aspects of the data set and publish findings in peer-reviewed journals. Clinical (blood and physical) studies are part of the data set, as are research diet histories that are evaluated using standard nutrient content of foods tables developed by USDA. While in national surveys we can't easily examine how the apple of one person compares with that of a second, we can compare estimates of the nutrient density of diets and gross differences in nutrient quality. While not the most exacting assessment for individuals, for population groups this method works well.

Information on the differences between conventional and organic produce comes from several studies in the United States and Britain involving chemical comparisons of nutrient differences in matched samples of produce. Consistently, they show organic produce with about 30 percent higher nutrient levels. The only time blood tests are done are when people are under treatment for specific disorders or are being monitored for the same. Blood tests are expensive and have limited predictive value in nutrition.

That is why I stress buying and eating organic and fresh produce. Natural foods are not standardized like vitamins. They vary in nutritional levels, but if you eat a variety of fresh, whole, organic foods you are likely to meet all of your nutritional needs. The same can't be said for commercial foods, to which synthetic nutrients have been added back to replace some (not all) of those lost in processing. But synthetic nutrients are not as bioactive as natural ones, so they may not do that much for you. While I don't think you need to look up the nutritive value of every morsel you put in your mouth, you should check to make sure you're getting enough and the right balance of nutrient-dense foods. The Guide to Healthy Eating is a tool for doing that. If you're eating at least the minimum number of servings suggested in this guide most days of the week, you probably are getting what you need.

- **Stock your cupboards and refrigerator with healthy fats.** Choose extra virgin olive oil; cold-pressed, pure-pressed, or expeller-pressed mono oils (peanut or canola) and vegetable oils (corn, safflower, soy); omega-3 oils (flaxseed oil); organic coconut oil; and organic salad dressings made from these healthy fats. If you use mayonnaise, make sure it is made of expeller-pressed oil and contains no trans-fats, partially hydrogenated, or hydrogenated fats. Store fats and oils in airtight containers in the refrigerator or in another cool dark place to prevent oxidation (rancidity). Throw out any oils or fats that look or smell not right. They're probably rancid, and consuming rancid oils is damaging to your health. *Do not cook with expeller-pressed vegetable oils, extra-virgin olive oils, flaxseed, or other omega-3 oils, as cooking destroys their fragile, beneficial chemistry.* Note: Olive is my choice, but some people like peanut or canola if it's organic and not GMO, as are most if not all commercial soy and canola oils. These are high monounsaturated oils with better heat tolerance (less likely to break down chemically) than most polyunsaturated oils.

- **Keep supplies of healthy snacks on hand.** Organic dried fruits, 100 percent whole-grain crackers (Ak Mak, Ryvita), 100 percent whole-wheat pita bread, nuts, beans (dry or canned), and bean, nut, and seed pastes (hummus, tahini, sunflower seed butter) are good snacks to stock.

- **Purchase good quality proteins.** Organic nut butters, a variety of nuts and seeds, canned tuna and salmon, and shelf-stable organic tofu products are good choices. Stock organic dairy foods (yogurt, hard and curd cheeses, milk), organic meats and poultry, coldwater wild fish, organic eggs, tofu, and tempeh.

- **Incorporate healthy herbs and spices into your diet.** Pick your favorite fresh or freeze-dried, non-irradiated, organic herbs and spices and store them in a cool, dry, dark place or in your freezer in airtight containers.

- **If you use soy products, make sure they're made with whole, organic soy, not conventionally**

processed and genetically modified (GM) soy.
Use small amounts, as they do in Asia, and also lean
toward the types eaten there: whole, fermented soy
in the form of tofu, tempeh, or other similar products. Fermented soy can contain more pesticide
residues than organic soy. GM beans are the worst
because they contain more antinutrient trypsin
inhibitors, lectins, and have higher allergenic potential—although all soybeans have some.

Soy is now one of the top eight causes of food
allergies, along with milk, eggs, peanuts, tree nuts,
fish, shellfish, and wheat. Soy is a hidden ingredient
in almost 70 percent of processed foods. The only
way to avoid it in food is to follow the ten rules in
this book and make your own meals and snacks. If
you suffer from food allergies, menstrual problems, a
thyroid disorder, infertility, digestive, or immune
problems, you're better off avoiding soy products
completely, especially soy oils and protein concen-
trates and isolates. Try miso, natto, and organic tofu.
For an excellent review of the subject, refer to *The
Whole Soy Story: The Dark Side of America's Favorite
Health Food* by Kaayla T. Daniel, Ph.D., CCN (New
Trends Publishing).

• **Green your larder.** Store in the fridge a variety of
organic fresh fruits and vegetables that you can use up
within a week. Most of us don't live far enough from
civilization that we have to worry about keeping
enough provisions on hand to last us through a hard
winter or hurricane season. Fresh organic foods are
the most nutritious, so it is best to shop frequently for
small amounts of these.

Menu Ideas

However much people want to improve their eating habits, where they seem to get stuck is on what to eat for breakfast, lunch, and dinner. "Tell me what I can eat for breakfast," one desperate client implored me, after she learned that the commercial breakfast cereal she had relied on for decades wasn't the best choice for her first meal of the day.

Here are seven days' worth of breakfast, lunch, and dinner menus designed to satisfy even the pickiest eaters.

BREAKFAST 1
Scrambled eggs with grated cheese and chopped
　　spinach
⅔ cup strawberries
Beverage

BREAKFAST 2
½ cup cottage cheese (whole)
1 slice whole-grain toast
1 tablespoon peanut butter
Beverage

BREAKFAST 3
Lean sliced turkey
1 tablespoon mayo on 2 Ak Mak or Ryvita crackers
Beverage

BREAKFAST 4
½ cup unsweetened yogurt (not low-fat)
¼ cup cottage cheese

½ cup berries or chopped apple or pear
Beverage

BREAKFAST 5
Scrambled eggs or tofu with onions, red peppers,
    and mushrooms
½ cup brown rice
Wedge of melon
Beverage

BREAKFAST 6
6-ounces old-fashioned oatmeal (not instant)
1 tablespoon dried raisins
1 tablespoon chopped nuts (walnuts, almonds)
1 teaspoon raw honey
¼ teaspoon cinnamon
Beverage

BREAKFAST 7
Melted mozzarella cheese topped by tomato slice
1 slice whole-grain bread
Small cluster of red grapes
Beverage

Lunches

Most of us eat some lunches away from home, either
brought from home or at a favorite lunch spot. Although
menus in fast-food restaurants have been "liberalized" to
contain some salads, fruits, and broiled items, their stock
in trade is still the factory foods they are famous for serv-

ing. The ingredients in a few popular fast-food items are listed here.

- **Chicken McNuggets.** Boneless chicken breast, water, modified cornstarch, salt, chicken flavor [yeast extract, salt, wheat starch, natural flavoring (animal source), safflower oil, dextrose, citric acid, rosemary], sodium phosphates, seasoning (natural extractives of rosemary, canola, and/or soybean oil, mono- and diglycerides, and lecithin). Battered and breaded with water, enriched bleached wheat flour (flour, niacin, reduced iron, thiamine mononitrate, riboflavin, folic acid), yellow corn flour, bleached wheat flour, modified corn starch, salt, leavening (baking soda, sodium acid pyrophosphate, sodium aluminum phosphate, monocalcium phosphate, calcium lactate), spices, wheat starch, whey, corn starch. Breading set in vegetable oil. Cooked in partially hydrogenated vegetable oils (may contain partially hydrogenated soybean oil, partially hydrogenated corn oil, partially hydrogenated canola oil, cottonseed oil, sunflower oil, and/or corn oil). Ingredients in the chicken portion include hydrolyzed corn gluten, lactose, soy and wheat gluten proteins, MSG, maltodextrin, modified cornstarch, partially hydrogenated soybean and cottonseed oil, dextrose, lactic acid, and silicon dioxide.

- **Cheeseburgers.** Fast-food hamburgers can contain as many as one hundred-thirteen different pesticide residues, according to the FDA, and trans-fatty acids (industrial fat). The American or cheddar-style cheese contains cultured pasteurized milk, salt, enzymes, artificial colors, powdered cellulose added to prevent caking, natamycin (a natural mold inhibitor), sodium citrate, and may contain less casein (cheese protein) and more starch, genetically modified ingredients, cheese cultures, salt, enzymes, sodium phosphate, sorbic acid, phosphoric acid, and artificial colors. The hamburger bun contains corn syrup, mono- and diglycerides, sodium stearoyl lacylate, polysorbate 60, calcium iodate, and wheat gluten.

- **Fast-food french fries.** These fries are made of potatoes, partially hydrogenated soybean oil, natural flavor (beef source), dextrose, and sodium acid pyrophosphate (to preserve natural color). They are cooked in partially hydrogenated vegetable oils that may contain partially hydrogenated soybean oil, partially hydrogenated corn oil, partially hydrogenated canola oil, cottonseed oil, sunflower oil, and/or corn oil.

- **Ketchup packets.** Ingredients are tomato concentrate from red ripe tomatoes, distilled vinegar, high fructose corn syrup, corn syrup, water, salt, and natural flavors (vegetable source).

From this mini review you can see that fast foods are a source of refined sugars, industrial fats, many synthetic chemicals you can live without, and more carbohydrates than you probably realized. Salads vary in carbs as well as other ingredients. A McDonald's Caesar salad with grilled chicken has only eleven grams of carbohydrate in a 10-ounce serving, but the same size California Cobb salad with crispy (breaded, fried) chicken has 48 grams, so choose carefully.

Many informal restaurants have salad bars and allow customers to load their plates with everything from greens to grains to grapes. It's usually a good bargain and a great way to help meet your daily quota of vegetables and fruits. But be careful about the extras; keep a lid on the creamy dressings and watch how many bacon bits you add to your plate.

Go for clear dressings or make your own from vinegar and olive oil, and if you just must have the blue cheese dressing, keep to one small ladle. Commercial blue cheese dressings are made of corn syrup, maltodextrin, high fructose syrup, xanthan gum, color, propylene glycol alginate, fumaric acid, potassium sorbate, disodium EDTA, BHT, disodium inosinate, and disodium guanylate. Enough said?

Here are a variety of lunches for those busy weekdays and hectic weekends.

Monday Lunch
1 small bowl of Cobb salad with grilled chicken, nitrate-free bacon, hard-boiled egg, crumbled blue cheese, salad greens, tomatoes, onions, cucumbers, radishes
2 tablespoons olive oil and vinegar dressing
1 medium size peach or apple
Beverage

Tuesday Lunch
1 scoop chicken salad on a bed of greens, mushrooms, cucumbers, tomatoes, sprouts, and onions
Two whole-grain crackers with 1 pat butter
⅔ cup fresh sliced strawberries with unsweetened cream
Beverage

WEDNESDAY LUNCH

1 turkey burger patty with mayo, lettuce, and sliced
  tomato on a whole-grain roll
Side green salad with oil and vinegar dressing
Wedge of honeydew melon
Beverage

THURSDAY LUNCH

Bowl of vegetable chili with 1 tablespoon grated
  cheddar cheese
Small square of cornbread
Small cluster of red grapes
Beverage

FRIDAY LUNCH

A medium bowl of chef salad with greens, roast beef,
  swiss cheese, hard-boiled egg, tomatoes, peppers
Olive oil vinaigrette
Small whole-grain roll
⅔ cup blueberries with unsweetened yogurt and
  honey
Beverage

SATURDAY LUNCH

1 portion zucchini quiche with whole-grain crust
Mixed green salad
2 tablespoons Russian dressing
1 medium baked apple
Beverage

SUNDAY BRUNCH

2-egg spinach, mushroom, and brie omelet
2 sausages

Fresh strawberry, orange, and pear slices
100 percent whole-grain or spelt bread cinnamon toast
Beverage

Fast and Easy Dinners

If you don't have the time or energy to tackle dinner from scratch and consider delivery a godsend, try these fast, fresh alternatives and compare. With the right ingredients on hand and a clear idea of what you are planning to make for dinner (plus leftovers), it's easy!

Mix and match meals and snacks that suit your schedule, budget, and palate. The right combo for a day is what you choose. You'll need to add snacks and bigger portions for bigger appetites, but it's easy to add sides and extras to go along with these tasty meals.

DINNER 1
Stir-fry tofu or shrimp in sesame oil with broccoli,
  onions, sprouts, and diced almonds
Brown rice
Spinach salad with mushrooms and red pepper
  dressing
Tangerine or orange wedges
Green tea

To make red pepper dressing, poach two whole red peppers in boiling water until soft. Cut into pieces, discarding the skins and inner seeds and membranes. Blenderize in your favorite Italian or vinegar and oil dressing.

DINNER 2
1 broiled chicken breast

Green beans sautéed in olive oil with a pinch of tarragon or sage

2 baked acorn squash wedges drizzled with maple syrup

Small cucumber and tomato salad with 2 tablespoons vinaigrette dressing

½ cup fresh fruit (apples, pears, and raspberries) plain or with a tablespoon of unsweetened cream

Beverage

DINNER 3
5-ounces steak fajitas with onions, red and green peppers, grated Monterey Jack cheese, tomatoes, lettuce, 1 tablespoon sour cream, and 1–2 tablespoons guacamole on a corn tortilla

½ cup fresh cubed pineapple

Beverage

DINNER 4
6-ounces broiled seasonal fish (from the sea, not a fish farm)

3–4 roasted baby potatoes drizzled with olive oil, chopped garlic, and rosemary

½ cup homemade coleslaw with shredded red and green cabbage, carrots, and onions, with a mayonnaise/sour cream/vinegar dressing containing black caraway seeds (optional)

1 wedge fresh watermelon, small bowl cherries, or 2 purple plums

Beverage

DINNER 5
Turkey breast stroganoff
Whole-wheat or buckwheat noodles or brown rice
Steamed asparagus
Mixed green salad with olive oil vinaigrette dressing
Apple
Beverage

In a slow cooker, throw in 2 cups cooked cubed turkey, 1 cup sliced mushrooms, ⅓ cup sliced onions, 2 cups slightly cooked broccoli florets, 1 cup chicken broth, ¼ teaspoon rosemary, salt and pepper. Cook until broccoli is tender. Make a sauce with 1 tablespoon butter, 3 tablespoons flour, broth from casserole, whisk thoroughly, then add 1 cup sour cream. When thoroughly heated and blended, pour over turkey and serve over noodles or rice.

DINNER 6
Meat loaf made with brown rice or whole-wheat
   crumbs
Whipped mashed cauliflower
Spicy stewed greens cooked in 2 tablespoons olive oil
Ripe pear, walnuts, and assortment of cheeses
Beverage

Snacking on the Run

What should you eat when you can't wait for the next meal and the only choices you can find come in a wrapper or a can? Here is a list of healthy snacks some of which require refrigeration. I keep a small plastic bag of almonds in my purse for occasions when I need a snack "fix" in order to last through the next event.

NO-CHILL SNACKS

2 tablespoons sunflower seeds, cashews, almonds, walnuts, pistachios, pumpkin seeds

1 apple, small cluster grapes, ¼ cup berries, ½ cup cubed cantaloupe or pineapple,

2 tablespoons raisins, 1 tangerine, 3 apricots (sulfite-free)

1–2 tablespoons nut butter with celery or carrot sticks

CHILLED SNACKS

2 tablespoons cottage cheese

1-ounce string cheese

1 deviled egg

2 tablespoons hummus with 2–3 whole-grain crackers

6-ounces yogurt with chopped fruit, dates, nuts

2 tablespoons almond or peanut butter with apple slices

5–6 marinated, grilled tofu squares

2 slices (2 ounces) cooked turkey or chicken breast

A Week's Worth of Healthy Eating

The upcoming seven sample menus are built around the "Ten Rules for Healthy Eating" in Chapter 2 and the Guide to Healthy Eating in Chapter 4. The menus are planned around 1,600 to 2,000 calories a day, which leaves "wiggle room" for bigger appetites to add occasional desserts or bigger portions. To lose weight, if that's your interest, you'll probably need to stick to about 1,600 calories for women or 1,800 calories for men. But especially when you're dieting, you should try to eat the minimum number of servings in the Guide to Healthy Eating daily.

If you're one of the people who find it difficult to eat all the recommended fruit and vegetable servings daily, you might want to keep a fruit and vegetable diary for a week. Make a note of the types and numbers of fruits and vegetables you eat every day. See if you are eating a rainbow of colorful fruits and vegetables each week: blue, purple, dark green, red, yellow, orange. These natural colors are associated with different powerful antioxidants. There are thousands of chemical antioxidants that protect us from toxins and metabolic wastes and boost our immunity. Some work inside of cells, some outside, and many work together synergistically. So for optimal health, you need to eat a rainbow of natural colors. Variety is your best protection! Eat different whole grains, meats, vegetables, and fruits each week, and choose natural fats, which are important to staying healthy and looking good.

Sample Menus

You can mix up these meals and snacks and substitute ingredients you like for ones you don't, as long as they are roughly comparable in protein, carbohydrate, and fat. Look up their food values in a book of food counts or use a food calculator on the Internet. Use these menus as models when you're planning what to eat out or take to work. Use them, too, when planning provisions for a long road trip. Recipes for dishes marked with an star (★) are in Chapter 6.

Don't leave out anything, even salad dressing. You need some fat in your diet. Don't worry, real olive oil won't make you fat as long as you don't overdo it. Low-fat dressings often have more sugars and carbohydrates, which are not great tradeoffs for weight-conscious people.

SUNDAY
Brunch
Smoothie: 1 cup milk with ½ cup unsweetened,
   frozen berries, ½ banana
1 poached egg
½ whole-wheat bagel
1 tablespoon cream cheese
2 orange wedges
Water, tea, or coffee

Dinner
4-ounces roast chicken, without the skin
Steamed green beans
Small sweet potato
Mixed green salad
2 tablespoons Italian dressing

Dessert
½ cup fresh fruit salad topped with shredded,
   unsweetened coconut

Snack
Raw vegetable sticks
Chili dip

MONDAY
Breakfast
1 pear
2 tablespoons peanut butter on 2 whole-grain crackers
1 cup milk

Lunch
1 cup lentil soup
Chicken salad stuffed tomato on large green salad

Dinner
*Beef with Chinese-Style Vegetables
½ cup brown rice
1 quartered orange

Dessert
2 slices *Banana Nut Bread with 2 teaspoons butter
Herbal tea or coffee substitute

TUESDAY
Breakfast
½ cup unsweetened frozen or fresh strawberries
½ small banana
6-ounces unsweetened yogurt
Water, tea, or coffee

Lunch
Large chef salad with 1-ounce cheese, 1-ounce turkey,
    1-ounce ham or roast beef
2 tablespoons Italian dressing
1 slice whole-grain bread
Water, herbal tea, or coffee substitute

Snack
½ apple with 1-ounce cheddar cheese

Dinner
Sliced ★Chicken Breast with Red Pepper Sauté
½ cup whole-wheat pasta
½ cup cooked fresh zucchini
Mixed green salad
2 tablespoons Italian dressing
5-ounces red wine (or alcohol-free red wine)
Tangerine

Dessert
Milk
2 graham crackers

WEDNESDAY
Breakfast
1 wedge honeydew or other melon
¼ cup cottage cheese
1 small corn muffin
1 teaspoon butter
½ cup milk

Snack
Tangelo or small orange

Lunch
Tossed salad with greens, sprouts, carrots, green
    onions
2 tablespoons Italian dressing

Grilled open-faced sandwich: 1-ounce ham and
    1-ounce cheese on 1 slice dark rye bread
Water, tea, or coffee substitute

Dinner
4-ounces *Flounder Florentine
½ cup brown rice
½ cup green peas (frozen)
1 wedge baked acorn squash
Water, herbal tea, or coffee substitute

Dessert
½ cup vanilla yogurt mixed with blueberries and
    raspberries (frozen or fresh, unsweetened)

THURSDAY
Breakfast
½ fresh grapefruit
½ cup oatmeal (not instant) + 1 tablespoon raisins,
    ¼ teaspoon cinnamon, and 1 teaspoon honey, milk
    to taste
Water, herbal tea, or coffee substitute

Midmorning Snack
2 slices turkey
2 teaspoons light mayonnaise
2 whole-grain crackers
1 cup milk

Lunch
Salad with mixed greens, walnuts, beets, goat cheese
1 tablespoon vinaigrette dressing with olive oil
Small whole-grain roll

1 teaspoon butter
Water, herbal tea, or coffee substitute

Snack
Fresh apple slices with 2 tablespoons peanut butter

Dinner
1 cup ★Vegetable Chowder
★Baked Fish with Spicy Sauce
Fresh steamed broccoli spears
Small wedge baked butternut squash
Small cluster seedless grapes

Dessert
1 small slice ★Gingerbread with 1 teaspoon butter
2-ounces unsweetened applesauce
Water, herbal tea, or coffee substitute

FRIDAY
Breakfast
½ cup fresh or canned unsweetened pineapple
½ cup homemade oatmeal with cinnamon and raisins
½ cup milk
Water, tea, or coffee

Snack
2 rye crisp crackers with 1-ounce cheese

Lunch
1 ★Beef or Turkey Taco
¾ cup fresh fruit cup: oranges, apples, bananas
½ cup vanilla yogurt

Dinner
4-ounces roast loin of pork (lean)
½ cup collard greens, kale, or chard
Tossed mixed salad
2 tablespoons Italian dressing
Water, herbal tea, or coffee substitute

Dessert
6-ounces apple cider
2-ounces peanuts (unsalted)

SATURDAY
Breakfast
6-ounces orange juice
2 ★Whole-Wheat Pancakes
2 tablespoons ★Blueberry Sauce
½ cup milk

Lunch
Tuna salad on 2 slices of whole-grain bread with
    sliced tomato, lettuce
Small green salad with 2 tablespoons Italian dressing
Water, iced tea (unsweetened)

Dinner
1 ★Chicken Breast Parmesan
Steamed spinach or arugula
½ cup whole-wheat spaghetti
5-ounces red wine (with or without alcohol)

Dessert
1 medium pear with ⅓ cup vanilla ice cream topped
    with frozen or fresh unsweetened raspberries

Snack
Herbal tea
1-ounce mixed nuts

More Tips to Help You Eat Well

The following ideas will also help you establish good eating habits.

- **Don't skip meals.** It can make you ravenously hungry and more likely to grab anything in sight.

- **Drink up.** Drink plenty of water. It will help you feel energized and full and enable you to stay away from beverages that increase your junk food cravings, such as diet soft drinks.

- **Don't go there.** Don't believe ads that "sell" the idea that you can eat factory-altered bread, pasta, and sweets and not suffer the consequences. Stick to real food.

- **Be brave.** You're entitled to ask a restaurant how menu items are prepared so you can decide if they are right for your health. After all, you're paying for them. Doesn't that mean you're in charge?

Chapter 6 provides some fast and easy recipes for some of the dishes used in the menus in this chapter as well as additional recipes and ideas for cooking with fresh and healthy foods.

What to Cook

Rosy potatoes in their tender skins, asparagus tips, pod-peas, beans two-inches long and slender as thick hairs, cooked to fresh perfection and dressed in a discreet veil of oil and condiments.

—M. F. K. Fisher

Many women learn how to boil water almost mystically when they get married, says M. F. K. Fisher, one of the world's great food writers, as if that blissful state brings with it new wisdom slipped on with the wedding ring. In my case I learned to cook from my mother, or I should say, because of my mother.

Mother was a Southern girl who prided herself on bringing to the table beautifully decorated dishes dressed in a colorful confetti of fruit bits and greens. She liked cooking roasts and salads using a small repertoire of condiments that included garlic, onion, carrot shreds, dill weed, pickling spice, ketchup, mustard, lemon, salt, and pepper, but her artful arrangements tasted bland, the meat overdone and the flavor boiled out of the vegetables.

When I was thirteen, I proposed that my parents let me take over the kitchen for a weekend so I could try my hand at dishes that were more adventurous. I used my small allowance to purchase some fresh herbs, spices, and cooking wines. I can't remember what I served, but it made my reputation as the cook in the family. From that point on, I was allowed a day a week to experiment in the kitchen, but mother always said she had to lock up the cooking wines when I took over.

As a result of these early recipe forays, when I married I wasn't afraid of the kitchen. In fact, fresh from our honeymoon, I asked my husband, who worked on Saturdays, what he liked to eat after work on weekends. He said, "something light." The lightest thing I could think of was a soufflé, so that is what I prepared for dinner the first night in our new home.

My husband, Jack, was stunned to be presented with a dish he'd only enjoyed in fine restaurants before. Of course he loved it, but he explained, laughing, that a soufflé wasn't what he meant by light. To him, light meant food prepared without a lot of fuss; leftover salads, cold cuts, cheese. By light he meant quickly served food, while I took it to mean air-filled and puffy, which only goes to show that each of us learns a different food language and culture.

When we think of pleasurable meals and dishes, some of us remember long hours in the kitchen chopping, blending, and heating. We don't think of quickly made meals, yet most of us depend on them for daily fare. We've been programmed to think of quick meals as part fresh and part what comes out of a package. My mother loved to make casseroles because that meant she could add a can of french-fried onions or dehydrated onion soup to spice up the flavor. In those days, savor came from condiments added from a can or bottle because that was what the home economist recipe developers at *Good Housekeeping, Family Circle,* and Betty Crocker advised. Today, few home cooks rely on canned onion rings for flavor, but spicing things up still means adding flavors from a bottle.

Now, you are more likely to look for quick dinner ideas in magazines like *Cooking Light, Eating Well,* and *Gourmet.* Their taste standards, like yours, are more sophisticated than those of our mothers. Now, chipotle chilies in adobo sauce are suggested to add fire to macaroni and cheese and chicken stew, as south of the border "hots" replace ketchup and tomato paste as recipe flavor boosters. But packaged or fresh, lean meals made fast are the standard.

Grilled marinated chicken breasts and pasta salad is the way Betty Crocker does fast and easy today. *Eating Well* magazine offers Shrimp Enchiladas Verde, a healthy, quick meal that starts with several convenience (read store-bought) ingredients. But Alice Waters, one of America's greatest chefs, has a different view of what's good to eat for dinner.

"A good kitchen respects its sources, chooses ingredients that are sound, seasonal, local when possible, and appropriate. Garnish and presentation play supplemental roles, not principal ones." Waters says respect for traditions is as important as creativity and inventiveness in cooking. We all have our own traditions, and we can trust that those time-honed recipes won't steer us wrong. Can tradition and quick, easy recipes go together without store-bought convenience? My answer is yes, most of the time.

This chapter offers some of my favorite easy and fast recipes that are consistent with the "Ten Rules for Healthy Eating." They emphasize nutrient-dense, antioxidant, and fiber-rich foods that most of us need more of and downplay ingredients we are wise to limit or avoid. But most important, they are delicious, easy, fast, and mostly fresh. Occasionally, a time-saving shortcut ingredient like frozen spinach or canned tomatoes is called for, but they are relatively innocuous ones in terms of health risks. However, you may choose to replace these commercial ingredients with fresh ones.

Later in this chapter you will find a vegetable seasoning guide. This is intended for people with FV (fear of vegetables) whose experience in the spice section of the supermarket is to feel overwhelmed. If you are a spice and herb avoider, try this challenge: for one week, dress your vegetables with one or several of the seasonings listed in the "Vegetable Seasoning Guide" sidebar. While fresh vegetables may be available some months of the year, there will be times when they're not available. Flavor is a highly perishable commodity. It starts to be lost moments after picking. In the months when most produce comes to us from storage, you'll want to perk up the flavor of your vegetables. Our need for nutrition doesn't take a winter break.

I invite you to use your creativity to improve these recipes. They are not ones you are likely to find in *Gourmet Magazine*. If you want fancier recipes, there are plenty of places on the Internet and in bookstores to find them.

Consider these recipes a starter set for when you're out of ideas for what to make or too bored, preoccupied, or tired to fuss.

The stated portion sizes may be too small for hearty appetites, so feel free to adjust portion sizes. Instead of four to six servings, recipes may serve two to three in your family. You be the judge. But food is not just something you eat. It's something you share.

Two years ago, four hundred families in Minneapolis did something outrageous; they promised to eat dinner together at least four times a week. Why was that so radical? It went against all trends. These parents opted for meals with their kids because research shows that kids who eat meals with their family have higher grades and are better adjusted than those who don't. They are less likely to use alcohol or marijuana, smoke, or feel depressed. They also eat more healthfully and have fewer weight problems; consuming more fruits and vegetables and less soft drinks and snack foods. Some people call the need for connection around food the social vitamin, because we have a biological need not only to eat but also to eat together.

Appetizers

Dilly Dip Veggies

Here is what Someday Farm, one of the first organic produce farms in Vermont, offers at its farmstand to tempt children to discover the joys of eating raw fresh organic vegetables.

Dipping Vegetables
Green salad leaves
Cucumber slices
Carrot sticks
Celery sticks
Green beans

Dilly Dip
½ cup plain yogurt
½ cup sour cream
¼ cup minced fresh herbs (dill and others)
1 tablespoon vinegar
½ teaspoon sea salt, tamari, or soy sauce
Water as needed

Dip with a Bite
½ cup extra-virgin olive oil
¼ cup red wine vinegar
2 tablespoons lemon juice
½ teaspoon mustard
2 tablespoons minced fresh herbs (parsley, dill, chives, or others)

Wash vegetables and gently pat dry. Pour each set of dip ingredients into a small jar with a lid. Shake well. Add a small amount of water for the right consistency, if needed. Serve each dip in a small bowl on a platter surrounded by vegetables for dipping.

Tip: Use the freshest ingredients for the best tastes and nutrition.

Hummus

I first tasted this recipe at a workman's café in an old Arab market. It was brought to the table warm with freshly baked small loaves of pita bread and a plate of assorted olives, pickled turnips, and hot peppers. Garnished with warm whole chickpeas, it was fragrant and delicious, despite the modest surroundings of brown-paper-covered tables bearing paper plates. It was far better than the factory-made hummus found in the chill cases of most supermarkets today.

> *1 medium can cooked chickpeas, with liquid*
> *1 clove garlic*
> *¼ cup tahini (sesame seed paste)*
> *Juice of ½ to 1 lemon to taste*
> *2 tablespoons extra-virgin olive oil*
> *Salt and pepper to taste*
> *Additional olive oil for drizzling*
> *1 tablespoon finely chopped fresh parsley*
> *Paprika*

In a saucepan, heat chickpeas and liquid from can over medium heat for 5 minutes. Cool to warm and pour into blender, reserving six to eight chickpeas for garnish. Add garlic, tahini, lemon juice, olive oil, and salt and pepper. Blend to puree consistency. Hummus should be white or lemony white in color. Pour the mixture into a wide, flat serving dish. Drizzle with a small amount of olive oil. Sprinkle with chopped parsley and paprika. Add reserved warm, whole chickpeas on top. Serve with Ak Mak crackers or whole-wheat pita bread triangles and a plate of Mediterranean-style olives and peppers.

Serves 3 to 4

Tip: Chickpeas, like all beans, greens, and whole grains, are not only high in fiber but also in folic acid, which has been found helpful in preventing Parkinson's disease.

Vegetarian Chopped Liver

This is a dish my mother used to make for parties that everyone loved and asked about. They could never guess what was in it. You'll be surprised how tasty, meaty, and flavorful this recipe is, and how much kids like it in sandwiches.

> 3 medium onions, sliced fine
> 3 tablespoons olive oil
> 3 hard-boiled eggs, shredded with a grater
> 2½ cups lightly cooked green beans
> ½ cup walnuts
> 2 tablespoons mayonnaise
> ½ teaspoon celery seed
> Juice of ½ to 1 lemon to taste
> Salt and pepper to taste
> Grated egg yolk, chopped parsley, or chopped scallions for
>   garnish and serve with endive leaves, celery stalks, cucum-
>   ber slices, or whole-wheat crackers

Sauté onions in olive oil. Allow to brown but not burn. Remove from pan and spoon into mixing bowl along with any oil left in pan. Add grated eggs and mix together. Set aside.

In a blender or food processor, purée beans, walnuts, mayonnaise, and celery seed. Pour into bowl with egg-onion mixture and blend together. Season with salt and pepper, dress with lemon juice, and garnish with grated egg yolk, chopped parsley, or scallions. Serve in endive leaves, celery stalks, or as a before-meal spread on cucumber slices, whole-wheat crackers, or in sandwiches.

Serves 3 to 4

Soups

Dutch Pea Soup

This recipe was the favorite of my cookbook editor, who said it tasted like the pea soup she remembered having in Holland. Since I'd never been to Holland at the time, I considered that a great compliment.

1 pound split peas, soaked overnight
1 ham bone (or ox tail or veal knuckle)
½ celery root, diced, or 3 outer stalks of celery, diced, plus 1
   teaspoon celery seed
2 leeks, diced
¼ cup diced celery tops
½ pound sausage or other savory meat, cubed
1 teaspoon dried thyme or 1 tablespoon minced fresh thyme
Salt and pepper to taste
¼ teaspoon dried basil or several fresh leaves torn or chopped

¼ teaspoon dried or a few torn or chopped fresh leaves sweet
*   marjoram*
Dash cayenne pepper or Tabasco
Toasted whole-wheat croutons

Boil peas in soaking water (plus enough added fresh water to total 2½ quarts), along with bone, in a soup kettle or heavy, 4–quart covered pot, for about 2 hours. Add diced vegetables and meat. Cook until vegetables are tender. Remove bone. Add salt, black pepper, basil, marjoram, and cayenne pepper or Tabasco. Simmer for a few minutes longer. Serve topped with croutons.

Yield: 6 servings of about 1 cup each

Tip: In addition to being an excellent source of fiber, dried peas are excellent sources of folic acid, vitamins A and C, and zinc.

Vegetable Chowder

A good way to use up leftover tidbits of vegetables, this is pretty much a bombproof recipe, and only 150 calories for a 1–cup serving.

1 onion, chopped
¼ cup chopped celery
2 tablespoons chopped green pepper
1 tablespoon olive oil
½ cup diced pared potatoes
1 cup corn kernels, fresh or frozen
½ cup green beans, fresh or frozen
½ cup diced yellow squash

1½ cups whole milk
2 tablespoons whole-wheat flour

In a 4-quart covered pot, cook onion, celery, and green pepper in olive oil until almost tender. Add potatoes, 1½ cups water, and seasonings. Cover and cook until potatoes are tender, about 20 minutes. Add corn, beans, and squash. Cover and cook for about 10 minutes or until beans and squash are tender. In a small bowl, mix flour with a small amount of milk. Add remainder of milk to cooked vegetable mixture, stir, then stir in flour-milk mixture. Cook over moderate heat, stirring constantly, until slightly thickened.

Yield: 4 servings of about 1 cup each

Tip: Substitute any root vegetable for potatoes, including rutabaga, turnips, carrots, parsnips, or sweet potatoes. You can also add your favorite herbs or spices. For herbs, try ¼ teaspoon tarragon or cilantro. For variations, try adding a pinch of turmeric or ½ teaspoon of curry powder to the chowder. One teaspoon of your favorite fresh herb combination, minced, would work, too.

Whole Grains

Whole-Wheat Pancakes

Use organic canola oil (non-GMO) to grease skillet, if needed
1½ cups whole-wheat flour
2 teaspoons baking powder

¼ *teaspoon salt*
1 *egg, slightly beaten*
1⅓ *cups whole milk*
1 *tablespoon brown sugar*
1 *tablespoon canola oil*

Grease skillet or use a well-seasoned one with a nonstick surface (not Teflon-coated). Heat griddle while mixing batter. When drops of water sprinkled on the griddle bounce, griddle is hot enough. Mix flour, baking powder, and salt. In a separate bowl, beat egg, milk, sugar, and oil together.

Add liquid mixture to flour mixture. Stir only until flour is moistened. Batter should be slightly lumpy. For each pancake, pour about ¼ cup batter onto hot griddle. Cook until covered with bubbles and edges appear slightly dry. Turn and brown other side. Serve with Blueberry Sauce.

Yield: 8 pancakes

Blueberry Sauce

2 *teaspoons cornstarch*
½ *cup water*
¾ *cup fresh or frozen unsweetened blueberries, thawed and crushed*
2 *tablespoons honey*
2 *teaspoons lemon juice*

Mix cornstarch with a small amount of water in a saucepan and stir until smooth. Add remaining water, blueberries, and honey. Bring to a boil over medium heat, stirring constantly. Cook until thickened. Remove from heat. Stir in lemon juice. Serve warm over pancakes.

Banana Nut Bread

1¾ cups whole-wheat flour
½ cup sugar
1 tablespoon baking powder
¼ teaspoon salt
½ cup chopped walnuts
⅓ cup canola oil
2 eggs
2 medium ripe bananas, mashed (about 1 cup)

Preheat oven to 350°F. Grease 9″ × 5″ × 3″ loaf pan. Mix flour, sugar, baking powder, salt, and nuts thoroughly. In a separate bowl, mix oil and eggs together. Mix in bananas. Add dry ingredients to banana mixture. Stir until just smooth. Pour into loaf pan. Bake 45 minutes or until firmly set when lightly touched in center top. Cool on rack. Remove from pan after 10 minutes.

Yield: 1 loaf; 18 slices

Cornbread

2 cups stone-ground cornmeal
1 tablespoon baking powder
¼ teaspoon salt
1 egg, slightly beaten

1 cup milk
2 tablespoons honey
¼ cup canola oil

Preheat oven to 400°F. Grease an 8-inch square baking pan. Mix cornmeal, baking powder, and salt thoroughly. In a separate bowl, mix egg, milk, honey, and oil. Add to cornmeal mixture. Stir only until dry ingredients are moistened. Batter will be lumpy. Pour into pan. Bake 20 minutes or until lightly browned.

Yield: 8 2" × 4" pieces

Tip: Stone-ground cornmeal is a whole grain.

Gingerbread

⅓ cup canola oil
⅓ cup water
⅓ cup light molasses
⅓ cup sugar
2 egg whites, slightly beaten
1 cup whole-wheat flour, unsifted
¼ teaspoon salt
¼ teaspoon baking soda
1 teaspoon baking powder
1 teaspoon ground ginger
½ teaspoon ground cinnamon
¼ teaspoon ground nutmeg

Preheat oven to 350°F. Grease an 8-inch square baking pan lightly with oil and flour. Mix oil and water. Add molasses, sugar, and egg whites. Stir until sugar is dissolved. Mix flour, salt, baking soda, baking powder, and spices. Add to liquid mixture and beat until smooth. Pour into pan. Bake 30 minutes or until surface springs back when touched lightly.

Yield: 8 2″ × 4″ servings

Entrées

Beef with Chinese-Style Vegetables

1 pound beef round steak, lean, boneless
⅔ cup green beans, cut in strips
⅔ cup thinly sliced carrots
⅔ cup thinly sliced turnips
⅔ cup thinly sliced cauliflower florets
⅔ cup Chinese cabbage, cut in strips
⅔ cup boiling water
2 teaspoons canola or peanut oil
4 teaspoons cornstarch
½ teaspoon ground ginger
⅛ teaspoon garlic powder
1 tablespoon soy sauce
3 tablespoons sherry (optional)
½ cup water

Trim fat from beef. Slice beef across the grain into strips about ⅛″ × 3″. (It is easier to slice meat thin if it is partially frozen.) Add vegetables to ⅔ cup boiling water. Simmer covered for 5 minutes or until vegetables are tender but still crisp. Drain. While vegetables are cooking, heat oil in nonstick frying pan. Add beef and stir-fry over moderately high heat, turning pieces of meat constantly until beef is no longer red, about 2 to 3 minutes. Mix cornstarch, ginger, garlic powder, soy sauce, sherry, and ½ cup water. Stir cornstarch mixture into beef. Heat until sauce starts to boil. Serve meat over vegetables.

Yield: 4 servings of ½ cup vegetables and ½ cup meat

Chicken Breast with Red Pepper Sauté

½ cup chopped red pepper
¼ cup boiling water
1 8-ounce can chopped tomatoes
½ cup tomato puree
1 clove garlic, whole
1 teaspoon fresh or ½ teaspoon dried oregano leaves
½ teaspoon celery seed
⅛ teaspoon black pepper
4 skinless chicken breast halves

Cook red pepper in boiling water until tender. Do not drain. Add tomatoes, tomato puree, garlic clove, oregano, celery seed, and black pepper to the red pepper. Simmer 10 minutes to blend flavors. Place breast halves in heavy skillet and pour tomato mixture over chicken. Cook, covered, over low heat until chicken is tender (about 60 minutes). Remove garlic clove before serving.

Yield: 4 servings of 1 breast

Flounder Florentine

1 pound skinless flounder fillets
1½ cups boiling water
1 10-ounce package frozen chopped spinach
1 tablespoon finely chopped onion
½ teaspoon dried marjoram leaves
1 cup milk
½ teaspoon salt
Dash pepper
2 tablespoons grated Parmesan cheese

Place fish fillets in 1 cup boiling water. Cook, uncovered, for 2 minutes. Drain. Place spinach and onion in ½ cup boiling water. Separate spinach with a fork. When water returns to boiling, cover and cook spinach for 2 minutes. Drain well. Mix with marjoram. Put spinach in 8-inch square glass baking dish. Arrange cooked fish on top of spinach. Mix flour thoroughly into ¼ cup of milk. Pour remaining milk in saucepan and heat. Add flour mixture slowly to hot milk, stirring constantly. Cook, stirring constantly, until thickened. Stir in salt and pepper. Pour sauce over fish and sprinkle with Parmesan cheese. Bake at 400°F until top is lightly browned and mixture is bubbly, about 25 minutes.

Yield: 4 servings of about 3 ounces of fish and ¼ cup spinach

Beef or Turkey Tacos

1 pound lean ground beef or turkey
¼ cup chopped onion

1 8-ounce can tomato sauce
2 teaspoons chili powder
1 cup chopped tomato
1 cup shredded lettuce
½ cup (2 ounces) shredded natural sharp cheddar cheese
12 taco shells

Brown ground beef or turkey and onion in a frying pan. Drain off any excess fat. Stir in tomato sauce and chili powder. Bring to a boil. Reduce heat and cook 10 to 15 minutes uncovered, stirring occasionally, until mixture is crumbly and dry. Fill taco shells with approximately 2 tablespoons of meat mixture. Mix tomato, lettuce, and cheese. Spoon about 2 tablespoons of mixture over beef in taco shells.

Yield: 6 servings of 2 tacos

Baked Fish with Spicy Sauce

1 pound fresh or frozen cod fillets, without skin
1 teaspoon olive oil, divided
¼ cup chopped onion
¼ cup chopped green pepper
1 8-ounce can whole tomatoes
¼ teaspoon salt
¼ teaspoon pepper

Thaw frozen fish. Grease 9-inch square baking pan lightly with ½ teaspoon oil. Cut fish into 4 pieces. Place in baking pan. Bake at 350°F until fish flakes easily, about 20 minutes. Drain cooking liquid from fish. While fish is baking, cook onions and green pepper in remaining oil until onion is clear. Cut up large pieces of tomatoes. Add tomatoes, salt, and pepper to cooked onions and green pepper. Cook 20 minutes to blend flavors. Pour sauce over drained fish. Bake 10 more minutes.

Yield: 4 servings of about 2½ ounces of fish

Chicken Breast Parmesan

1 pound chicken breasts (3–4)
½ cup mayonnaise (organic or trans-fat free)
¼ cup grated Parmesan cheese
1 tablespoon oregano

Place 1 pound chicken breasts (3–4) in a pyrex dish or pie pan. Combine ½ cup mayonnaise (organic or trans-fat free), ¼ cup grated Parmesan cheese, 1 tablespoon oregano. Mix well, and spoon over raw chicken breasts. Bake uncovered at 375°F for about one hour or until fork tender and no pink juices appear.

Yield: 4 servings of one chicken breast

Vegetable Dishes

A good way to get a regular supply of fresh produce is to buy a seasonal share in a local CSA (community-supported agriculture) farm. If you do this, or if you frequent a local farmer's market or a grocery that features

fresh produce, there will be times when you are con-
fronted with unfamiliar vegetables. Although there's no
way for me to know what these may be in your case, I've
included a few basic recipes for some unfamiliar vegetables
you are likely to find occasionally in your weekly allot-
ment of produce.

Mashed Kohlrabi

Kohlrabi has always looked to me like a space invader with
antennae growing out of a pale green bulbous ball of a
body. It's better known in Europe than America and quite
tasty, a mild cross between cabbage and celery.

2 cups cubed, cooked kohlrabi
2 tablespoons butter
⅓ cup whole milk
2 tablespoons grated onion
Salt and pepper to taste
¼ teaspoon ground nutmeg

To prepare, trim the tops and pare the bulbous root of the
kohlrabi. You can cook kohlrabi whole or cubed. Start by
boiling them in salted water, uncovered, till soft, about 30
minutes for the cubed and longer for whole ones.

Mash kohlrabi with a fork. Add butter, milk, onion, salt
and pepper, and nutmeg. Reheat in oven before serving.

Yield: 4 servings

Swiss Chard with Nuts and Raisins

> *2 bunches Swiss chard*
> *2 tablespoons olive oil*
> *1 small onion, chopped*
> *½ cup raisins*
> *¼ cup pignoli (pine nuts)*
> *1 teaspoon cinnamon*
> *Salt and pepper to taste*

Clean and remove large stems from chard. Cook for about 10 minutes, covered, in a small amount of water. Remove and drain well. Heat oil in skillet. Add onion, raisins, and pignoli. When pignoli are lightly browned and onions are soft, add chard and cook, covered, over moderate heat for about 15 minutes or until tender. Add cinnamon, salt, and pepper in last moments of cooking.

Yield: 4 servings

Rutabaga Pudding

This recipe was given to me by Scandinavian friends who said they ate it as children and looked forward to it each year during harvest season. Perhaps you and your children will look forward to it as well. Hardly seems possible? Just try it.

> *2 large rutabagas, peeled and diced*
> *¼ cup finely grated whole-wheat bread crumbs*
> *½ cup whole milk*
> *3 ounces melted butter*

2 eggs, well beaten
2 tablespoons molasses
¼ teaspoon mace
1 teaspoon salt
Dash pepper
1 teaspoon cinnamon sugar

Cook rutabagas, covered, in boiling, lightly salted water for about 20 to 30 minutes or until tender. Drain. Soak crumbs in milk. Mash rutabaga with butter. Combine eggs, molasses, and seasonings and fold into mashed vegetable. Add milk and crumbs and mix well. Pour into greased baking dish. Sprinkle top with cinnamon sugar. Bake at 375°F oven for about 1 hour.

Yield: 6 to 8 servings of about ⅔ cup

Cauliflower à la Grecque

This recipe also can be used with all the summer's bounty of vegetables: broccoli, snap beans, celery, brussels sprouts, mushrooms, squash, and carrots, and served as an appetizer, salad, or side dish accompanying an entrée.

1 head cauliflower
Boiling water to cover

Marinade
2 cups water
1 cup dry white wine
Juice of 2 lemons
2 tablespoons white vinegar

1 bay leaf
2 peppercorns
⅛ teaspoon thyme
1 heaping teaspoon fennel seed

Tip: For variation, add ⅓ cup olive oil to marinade before cooking.

Separate cauliflower into flowerets. Trim off outer leaves and tough stalk material. Wash thoroughly. Place in casserole dish. Pour over it enough boiling water to cover cauliflower, and cover baking dish. Allow cauliflower to steep in hot water for 5 minutes. Meanwhile, in a saucepan, heat marinade ingredients and bring to a slow boil. Simmer for a few minutes. Drain cauliflower and add to simmering mixture. Simmer for a few minutes until flowerets are tender but still crisp. Remove from heat and cool in marinade. Refrigerate until needed.

Yield: 6 servings

Beet Raita

If you see fresh beets at your local farmer's market or find a few in your share of weekly vegetables, be sure to try this recipe influenced by East Indian cuisine traditions.

1 pound medium size beets, cooked until tender and grated
1½ cups plain, whole-milk yogurt
1 small onion, grated
½ cucumber, grated

½ teaspoon chili powder
Salt to taste
Pinch of sugar

Mix ingredients together. Chill at least 1 hour before serving. Use as a relish-style accompaniment to your entrées.

Yield: 6 to 8 servings

Tip: Beets are an excellent source of folic acid.

Baked Onion Gumbo

2 pounds yellow onions, sliced
1 green pepper, diced
2 tablespoons chopped celery
3 ripe tomatoes, chopped
1 clove garlic, diced
½ teaspoon curry powder
½ teaspoon chili powder
Dash Tabasco
⅓ cup whole-wheat bread crumbs
2 tablespoons grated Parmesan cheese
1 tablespoon butter

Place onions in greased baking dish. Add green pepper, celery, tomatoes, garlic, and other seasonings. Mix bread crumbs with Parmesan cheese. Top onions with crumb mixture and dot with butter. Bake at 350°F for about 1 hour.

Yield: 4 to 6 servings

Note: Onions and garlic are potent factors in preventing cancers and inhibiting progression of cancers.

In Chapter 7, we explore nourishing your mind, body, and spirit. We all eat, yet we often do it with little conscious awareness of what we are eating or how it influences our health and wellness or our interactions and connections to the world in which we live. This chapter is designed to open your mind and senses to the subtle dimensions of diet and nutrition.

Vegetable Seasoning Guide

Use these herbs and spices to make eating vegetables an adventure. Each has special nutritional, health, and healing properties, and unique flavor properties. These are my favorites. You may find others to add to this list or to use in combinations.

- **Asparagus.** Basil, chive, coriander, dill, fennel, marjoram, nutmeg, oregano, savory, tarragon, thyme
- **Beans (snap).** Anise, basil, caraway, celery seed, chervil, chives, coriander, curry, dill, fennel, garlic, ginger, marjoram, mint, mustard, oregano, rosemary, sage, thyme
- **Beets.** Allspice, anise, basil, cinnamon, cloves, curry, cumin, dill, fennel, ginger, marjoram, mustard, nutmeg, poppy seed, sage, tarragon
- **Bell peppers.** Bay leaf, chili powder, curry, dill, fennel, garlic, ginger, mustard, oregano, sage, thyme

- **Broccoli.** Basil, celery seed, garlic, marjoram, mustard, oregano, savory, thyme
- **Brussels sprouts.** Basil, celery seed, cinnamon, curry, cumin, fennel, garlic, mustard, nutmeg, sage, tarragon, thyme
- **Cabbage.** Anise, basil, bay leaf, caraway, celery seed, cinnamon, cloves, curry, cumin, garlic, mustard, nutmeg, oregano, poppy seed, rosemary, sage, thyme
- **Carrots.** Allspice, anise, basil, caraway, celery seed, chervil, cinnamon, chili powder, chives, cilantro, cloves, coriander, curry, cumin, dill, fennel, ginger, marjoram, mint, mustard, nutmeg, oregano, poppy seed, rosemary, savory, tarragon, thyme
- **Cauliflower.** Anise, basil, caraway, chili powder, chives, coriander, curry, cumin, dill, fennel, garlic, marjoram, mustard, nutmeg, rosemary, sage, savory, thyme, turmeric
- **Celery.** Anise, basil, bay leaf, caraway, chervil, chili powder, chives, curry, cumin, dill, fennel, garlic, ginger, marjoram, mustard, nutmeg, oregano, poppy seed, poultry seasoning, savory, tarragon, thyme
- **Corn.** Allspice, anise, basil, celery seed, chervil, cinnamon, chili powder, chives, cloves, coriander, curry, cumin, dill, fennel, ginger, marjoram, nutmeg, oregano, rosemary, sage, savory, tarragon, thyme
- **Cucumbers.** Allspice, basil, celery seed, chives, dill, mint, mustard, oregano, tarragon, thyme

- **Eggplant.** Allspice, basil, celery seed, chili powder, coriander, curry, cumin, fennel, garlic, ginger, marjoram, mustard, nutmeg, oregano, sage, tarragon, thyme
- **Greens.** Allspice, anise, basil, chervil, coriander, curry, cumin, fennel, garlic, ginger, marjoram, nutmeg, oregano, rosemary, sage, savory, tarragon, thyme
- **Kohlrabi.** Allspice, caraway, chervil, cinnamon, coriander, curry, fennel, garlic, marjoram, mustard, nutmeg, poppy seed, rosemary, savory, thyme
- **Leeks.** Anise, bay leaf, celery seed, chervil, dill, fennel, ginger, marjoram, mint, mustard, nutmeg, rosemary, sage, tarragon, thyme
- **Lettuce.** Anise, basil, caraway, celery seed, chervil, chives, dill, garlic, mint, mustard, nutmeg, oregano, rosemary, sage, savory, tarragon, thyme
- **Mushrooms.** Allspice, anise, basil, bay leaf, celery seed, chervil, chili powder, coriander, curry, cumin, fennel, garlic, ginger, marjoram, mustard, nutmeg, oregano, rosemary, sage, savory, tarragon, thyme
- **Okra.** Chili powder, curry, garlic, ginger, mustard, oregano, savory, thyme
- **Onions.** Allspice, anise, bay leaf, chervil, cinnamon, chili powder, cilantro, cloves, coriander, curry, cumin, dill, fennel, garlic, ginger, marjoram, mustard, nutmeg, oregano, poppy seed, sage, savory, tarragon, thyme

- **Parsnips, turnips, and rutabagas.** Allspice, celery seed, cinnamon, clove, curry, cumin, garlic, ginger, mustard, nutmeg, tarragon
- **Peas.** Allspice, anise, basil, celery seed, chervil, chili powder, chives, coriander, curry, cumin, dill, fennel, garlic, ginger, marjoram, mint, mustard, nutmeg, oregano, rosemary, sage, savory, tarragon, thyme
- **Potatoes.** Allspice, chive, cinnamon, coriander, curry, cumin, ginger, mint, mustard, nutmeg, oregano, poppy seed, rosemary, sage, tarragon, thyme
- **Summer squash.** Basil, celery seed, cinnamon, chili powder, cilantro, coriander, curry, dill, fennel, garlic, ginger, marjoram, mint, oregano, rosemary, sage, tarragon, thyme
- **Sweet potatoes.** Allspice, anise, cinnamon, clove, coriander, curry, cumin, ginger, nutmeg, rosemary, savory
- **Tomatoes.** Basil, bay leaf, celery seed, chervil, chili powder, chives, curry, cumin, dill, garlic, ginger, marjoram, mint, mustard, oregano, rosemary, sage, tarragon, thyme
- **Winter squash.** Allspice, anise, cinnamon, clove, coriander, curry, cumin, ginger, nutmeg, rosemary, savory

7

Food, Mind, and Spirit

One cannot think well, love well, or sleep well if one has not dined well.

—Virginia Woolf

"Fish is brain food," I often heard my mother say when I was growing up. I didn't know if that was true or just her way of encouraging me to eat fish, a food that was unappealing to me. As an adult I discovered how enjoyable a dish of fish can be and how valuable nutritionally. It turns out fish really is brain food, but it's only recently that we found out why.

The foods you eat affect how your brain performs. Research shows eating the right foods can boost your IQ, improve your mood, make you more emotionally stable, sharpen your memory, and help you feel young. Fish figures in that picture because it is one of the complete protein foods whose amino acids can be converted into neurotransmitters, the chemicals that carry messages between the brain and the cells.

Your brain relies on protein to make neurochemicals, of which there are many, including a few that directly influence your appetite.

- **Serotonin.** This neurotransmitter is released after you eat sugars and starches. It is made from the amino acid tryptophan, one of the essential amino acids in foods. Serotonin makes you feel calm and brightens your mood. It is involved in relaxation, sleep, optimistic moods, appetite, cravings, and feelings of pleasure and arousal. People who have low levels of serotonin have difficulty sleeping and can be clinically depressed.

- **Dopamine and Norepinephrine.** These chemicals enhance mental alertness and concentration. Made from the amino acid tyrosine, all protein foods (fish, meat, milk products, nuts, beans, soy products) are rich in dopamine building blocks, which is why you feel more energized, alert, and assertive after eating protein foods.

According to Judith Wurtman, Ph.D., and her husband, Richard Wurtman, M.D., the scientists at MIT who first linked food and mood in the 1980s, what we know today about the food/mind/mood connection allows you to select foods that will "Power your brain, modify your moods, and make you a more effective, motivated, and possibly even a more contented individual." Somewhere between the fork and the lips, however, all of those worthy goals seem to get sandbagged.

Food and Mood

We've all had them at one time or another—an intense, unrelenting desire for pizza, a coke, a cheeseburger and fries, chocolate, or an ice cream sundae. We feel foolish and weak-kneed when we give in to these inner demons, but what are you going to do when the desire to sink your teeth into "something good" blunts your ability to concentrate on anything else?

Eating is one of the ways we deal with our emotions. When we feel bad, we try to control the bad feelings with food. We eat to derive immediate pleasure in order to stifle pain, confusion, fear, or unexpressed feelings of regret, guilt, and grief. Food, either drowning ourselves in it or punishing ourselves by restricting it, overwhelms the bad feelings and makes it seem, if but for a moment, that everything is okay.

Studies suggest that there is a biological explanation for why we seek out comfort foods when under stress. It is a chemical response of your brain to elevated levels of stress hormones. Here's how it works. When you eat a high-sugar, high-starch snack, the hormone insulin is released from your pancreas into the bloodstream. Insulin helps your cells absorb the excess sugar from the bloodstream. The cells then release the amino acid tryptophan, which travels via the bloodstream to the brain, where it is used to make serotonin. Tryptophan is the only essential amino acid that can be converted into serotonin, which, in turn, can be converted into melatonin, the sleep hormone. In the right amounts, serotonin makes us feel calm, in control, and able to handle stress, and it helps us have a good night's rest. When too much serotonin is released, you feel agitated and nervous, and with too little, you feel lethargic, hopeless, and unable to sleep.

Many drugs called serotonin selective reuptake inhibitors or SSRIs (including Prozac, Zoloft, and Paxil), used to treat depression, anxiety, and related emotional disorders work by increasing the amount of serotonin available to the cells. The right eating habits are the safest nonmedical way of balancing mood, sleep, and stress. (Consult your doctor before changing your use of any medications.)

If you'd like to try improving your sleep and mood by eating right, choose foods that are naturally rich in tryptophan. Seratonin is produced by the body during the digestion of tryptophan-containing foods. Tryptophan is an essential amino acid that is a part of many foods containing protein, such as milk, eggs, and meat. The body can't make its own seratonin, it has to come from food or supplements. You don't need a lot. A turkey sandwich and a whey protein shake are enough to get your daily needs met. People with low protein diets, like some vegetarians, may not get enough and may want to consider taking a supplement. Natural sources of tryptophan that vegetarians might consider include black-eyed peas, black and English walnuts, almonds, sesame seeds, and roasted pumpkin seeds.

Although most people have adequate amounts of tryptophan in their diets, people who've been dieting, especially on low-carbohydrate plans, may have low circulating levels of tryptophan, as do people with irritable bowel syndrome, discussed in Chapter 8. People undergoing certain treatments for cancer and people with chronically elevated levels of cortisol, the stress hormone, may also have low levels. Too little seratonin in your body is associated with moodiness, depression, poor and erratic sleep, binge eating, and other problems in appetite control.

Although tryptophan is present naturally in many foods, including turkey, chicken, fish, cottage cheese, bananas, eggs, nuts, wheat germ, avocados, milk, cheese, and legumes (beans, peas), the absorption of tryptophan is improved by eating a small amount of carbohydrate— brown rice or whole-grain bread—with tryptophan- containing protein foods.

Tryptophan is released during digestion. Some of it is taken up by cells in the wall of the intestines and stored as serotonin. The rest enters the bloodstream and circulates to the brain where it is taken up. The point is unless the tryptophan is released in the *gut* during digestion, as a result of some carbs being present along with tryptophan- containing foods, it cannot be carried to the brain where it can be picked up by brain cells. This is a great example of how nutrition, digestion, circulation, and metabolism interconnect. We tend to think of them as separate sys- tems, but that's not how it works in our bodies. It also demonstrates how nutrition influences functional health.

In practical terms, some people find that by taking tryptophan supplements (500 mg) in combination with a high-carbohydrate meal or snack helps them sleep more soundly, withstand jet lag, and feel more upbeat, generally.

Fat, Stress, and Weight

When the body gears up to deal with stress, two stress hormones, adrenaline and cortisol, are released to mobi- lize fat and carbohydrates stored in the body for the quick energy needed for the "fight-or-flight" reaction. Once the acute stress is over, adrenaline goes away but cortisol stays around to help refuel the body and bring it back into balance. One of the ways it does this is by giving you a raging appetite that drives you to replace the carbs and fats you've used up in the crisis. Even though our stresses today are more likely to be intellectual or emotional, our Paleolithic bodies still react to them as if we were about to do battle with a saber-toothed tiger.

Under chronic stress, levels of the adrenal hormone cortisol remain high, creating a buildup of abdominal fat, our primitive emergency energy supply, and suppressing thyroid function. Cortisol also has many other functions. It influences sugar control, has an anti-inflammatory effect, and aids immune system function. When our bodies confront stress, the adrenal glands secrete cortisol to divert energy to meet the increased needs of our muscles and brain to respond to the stress.

Normally, cortisol levels drop after the stressful event. But in modern times, when people often are pushed beyond their normal coping ability to handle stress, elevated cortisol levels become chronic, leading to many functional problems including depressed immune function, low thyroid function, problems with sugar control, and eventually, adrenal fatigue ("burnout"), and chronic illness. Stress eating and weight gain are the result of cortisol stimulating insulin, the hormone manager of fat stores, to promote fat storage.

People with adrenal exhaustion have toxic stress, says Pamela Peeke, M.D., an NIH researcher and author of *Fight Fat After Forty*. Adrenal exhaustion can have a life-threatening effect on your body, including increasing your

susceptibility to illness and impairing memory and concentration. Toxic stress stimulates higher than normal levels of cortisol, says Peeke, characterized by hopelessness
and helplessness. When the stress hormone stays high it
causes chronic increased appetite, which adds on extra
pounds. After forty, the extra pounds accumulate deep
inside the belly, below the abdominal muscle wall, stored
for the flight-or-fight reactions that we have little need of
today. What's more, with continued high cortisol levels
you are likely to develop metabolic syndrome, a complex
of health problems that include high blood pressure, high
heart rate, diabetes, and increased risk for stroke, blood
clotting, and colon cancer.

To turn off toxic stress reactions you have to first
reconceptualize your stresses, says Peeke. If you don't
sense them as stressful, you won't experience them that
way. Most of our stresses don't come from life-threatening
situations but from annoying but livable provocations: the
car that cuts you off on your way to work, the long line at
the bank, the mistake your credit card company made, and
the slow cashier at the grocery store. Things like that don't
have to contribute to toxic stress if in your mind you convert them to ABLs—annoying but livable stresses. If you
do, you can keep the level of cortisol below the appetite-
stimulating "jelly belly" level.

Second, when you feel angry or fragile after an
"assault" by your boss, your significant other, or the
copier machine, take a walk. It will help you to clear your
head and feel better. One thing you don't want to do is
respond with mindless eating, which, in response to stress,
is likely to be low-quality, high-sugar, and high-fat foods
that increase insulin levels. High insulin together with

high cortisol levels layer on deep belly fat. What your body needs you to do is not get fatter but more physical!

Women, Carbohydrates, and Mood Swings

Researchers are investigating the effects of eating carbohydrates on mood. Women's food cravings for carbohydrates, especially at puberty, before menstrual periods, during pregnancy, and after menopause, may be due to estrogen's influence on brain chemistry and blood sugar levels. It's thought that women may be more sensitive to changes in serotonin levels than men, and when estrogen levels fall and progesterone levels are high, serotonin levels drop, resulting in an increase in appetite, carbohydrate cravings, and weight gain. Scientists from the University of Michigan have been able to link the craving for sugary and fatty foods with these foods' ability to make people feel calm and cheerful. By this light, chocolate is an ideal de-stressor that is hard to resist.

We seem to crave high-fat, sugary foods to experience the benefits of endorphins, naturally occurring chemicals in the brain that produce pleasurable feelings and are natural painkillers. Chocolate not only has an ideal ratio of fat and sugar (50-50), it is rich in an endorphin-releasing compound called phenylethylamine. But does that mean women are stuck with an addiction to foods that cause weight gain? Fortunately no, you can get the same brain chemical high from whole-grain crackers and breads that also stabilize serotonin levels. To keep endorphin levels up, keep to a regular exercise program. If you can't get rid of your chocoholic urges, a small amount won't hurt and will probably be enough to satisfy your chocolate itch. But if a little is likely to lead to a lot, eat a small amount of a protein food instead—nuts, cheese, chicken—to make the urge go away.

Nutrients, Cravings, and the Brain

The brain is like a chemical factory that continuously produces chemical messengers, such as serotonin and dopamine, to tell the cells when to start, continue, or stop various biochemical reactions. The only raw materials used in this process are nutrients. Research has shown that if the brain doesn't get the right amounts and balance of nutrients an imbalance of neurotransmitters is produced that can slow down the body's processes or make its reactions chaotic.

Other research is focusing on the hypothalamus, the region of the brain that regulates hunger. It seems that obese people take longer to feel full. Delayed feelings of fullness are associated with greater weight gain, and researchers speculate that fullness signals from the gut to the brain may be delayed and weaker in obese people. If it takes ten minutes, normally, for a meal to be processed and a fullness signal to be received by the brain, then the longer it takes to eat a meal or snack, the better off you are, says Mark Gold, Ph.D., an addiction researcher at the University of Florida, who adds that no one should eat in less than ten minutes.

Other researchers are looking at other causes of cravings. People tend to binge when they've gone without food or have been on a restricted diet. Cravings may be a psychological reaction to wanting what you couldn't have, or they may result when your body is depleted in certain nutrients and needs these nutrients. Scientists' interest in the subject of food cravings is enhanced by their realization that you can't get rid of cravings, although you can gain control over them.

Surviving Stress

Acute stress shuts down digestive activity, but once the threat is over, stress hormones and digestion usually return to normal. Continuing stress can trigger numerous life-limiting disorders and conditions, from heart disease and gastroesophageal reflux disease (GERD) to irritable bowel, high blood pressure, and diabetes. An important factor in controlling stress and avoiding serious illness related to it is a healthy diet and lifestyle. Healthy eating, as recommended in the "Ten Rules for Healthy Eating" in Chapter 2, makes you more resistant to stress and able to recover from it more quickly and efficiently.

Nutrients That Combat Stress

Several nutrients are particularly important to managing stress well. Unfortunately, they tend to be underconsumed by many North Americans. They are highlighted here so you can be sure you are taking good sources of them daily.

Zinc

This essential mineral needed in small amounts is critical to our well-being. It is part of at least eighty different enzyme reactions, and it is believed to be a brain neurotransmitter. Zinc deficiency can result in some or all of the following symptoms: irritability, chronic anger, poor memory, growth retardation, impaired intellectual ability, weak immunity, joint pain, loss of taste and smell, acne, asthma, fertility problems, loss of virility, impaired wound healing, and inability to handle stress, among numerous other affects and reactions.

Good food sources of zinc include oysters, which contain more zinc per serving than any other food, red meats and poultry, beans, nuts, whole grains, and dairy products.

Copper

This essential mineral needed in very small amounts is a part of several enzyme systems and is a component of blood proteins. It helps to convert iron into hemoglobin, stimulates the growth of red blood cells, and is part of several digestive enzymes. It also helps the amino acid tyrosine to work as a pigment factor in hair and skin. Deficiency of copper results in physical weakness, digestive disturbances, and problems with breathing. Premature infants sometimes develop copper deficiency that shows up as chronic diarrhea and later, as anemia.

Excellent sources of copper are liver, oysters, clams, crab, cashews, sunflower seeds, hazelnuts, and almonds.

Peanut butter, lentils, beans, wheat bran cereals, whole grains, and mushrooms are good sources.

Vitamin B₆

B_6 is involved in more than one hundred different enzyme reactions of the body, including the reaction that converts the amino acid tryptophan to serotonin. It plays a vital role in the release of glucose from muscle glycogen and in the conversion of some amino acids to glucose. It affects the ability of red blood cells to carry oxygen throughout the body and limits the ability of steroid hormones, such as estrogen and progesterone, to bind to receptors in the cell nucleus, which protects against the development of breast and prostate cancers.

B_6 deficiency creates numerous neurological abnormalities including irritability, depression, and confusion. Other symptoms are tongue inflammation, mouth sores, and ulcers at the corners of the mouth. Alcoholics are most at risk for deficiency because of poor diets and impaired metabolism of the vitamin. Among nonalcoholics, low levels raise risks of heart disease, weakened immune function, Alzheimer's disease, and other conditions of intellectual decline.

Good food sources of vitamin B_6 include bananas, salmon, turkey, chicken, potatoes, and spinach. Most people in North America who eat plenty of protein and calories get enough B_6. Vegetarians should be careful to eat good sources daily or take a vitamin-mineral supplement.

Essential Fatty Acids (EFAs)

Omega-3 and omega-6 fatty acids, the two fatty acids we need to consume, are essential because they are involved in the functioning of every cell, tissue, and organ in the human body. The omega-6 EFAs are distributed evenly in most tissues, but omega-3 EFAs are concentrated in just a few tissues, such as the brain, in the form of DHA converted from omega-3. The brain has the highest percentage of fat of any other organ in the body—20 percent of the dry weight of the brain is made up of EFA/DHA. As with many vitamins, we can't make EFAs in our bodies so we must eat them, but unlike the vitamins that are needed in milligram and microgram amounts, we need EFAs in gram amounts.

The human body uses EFAs to manufacture and repair cell membranes, obtain needed nutrition, and expel harmful waste products. A primary function of EFAs is the production of prostaglandins, hormones that regulate heart rate, blood pressure, blood clotting, fertility, conception, and inflammation and encourage the body to fight infection. Essential fatty acids are also needed for proper growth in children, particularly for neural development and maturation of sensory systems, with male children having higher needs for EFAs than females. Fetuses and breast-fed infants must obtain an adequate amount of EFAs from their mother's diet.

EFA deficiency and imbalances have been linked to heart attacks, cancer, insulin resistance, asthma, lupus, schizophrenia, depression, postpartum depression, accelerated aging, stroke, obesity, diabetes, arthritis, ADHD, and Alzheimer's disease. Omega-3 deficiencies are related to decreased memory and mental abilities, tingling sensation of the nerves, poor vision, increased tendency to form blood clots, diminished immune function, increased triglyceride and bad cholesterol (LDL) levels, high blood pressure, irregular heart beat, menopausal discomfort, and growth retardation in infants and children.

Food sources of omega–3s include flaxseeds, walnuts, pumpkin seeds, Brazil nuts, sesame seeds, avocados, dark leafy green vegetables (kale, spinach, purslane, mustard greens, collards), canola oil (cold-pressed and unrefined), soybean oil, wheat germ oil, flaxseed oil, salmon, mackerel, sardines, anchovies, and albacore tuna. One tablespoon daily of flaxseed oil can provide for daily needs, but it might be more beneficial to eat food sources, such as nuts, more than once a day.

De-Stressing

You may be one of the millions of people who use chocolate, ice cream, or pizza to numb down their stressful feelings. Using food to de-stress tells the brain, "Now that you've made me pay attention and refuel with high-energy food, you can relax."

But there are other options besides eating to decrease stress. You can choose exercise, yoga, meditation, sex, or a warm bath, all of which activate your brain's pleasure centers and physically relieve stress. But we don't always remember we have these other options when we're in the middle of a stress flare-up that makes us reach for something to extinguish the fire.

Are there foods that can heal stress feelings? While there are no foods that will wipe away the causes of stress in your life, if you've been following the "Ten Rules for Healthy Eating," you are in good shape, nutritionally, so when you run into a wall of stress you will be well-fortified and have adequate reserves to deal with the crisis emotionally.

Here are a dozen things you can do to reduce stress levels and conquer cravings:

- **Wait ten minutes before giving in to a craving.** If you can distract yourself for ten or fifteen minutes by answering e-mails, playing with the cat, helping your kids do homework, or running an errand, you may forget about it.

- **Never go hungry.** Hunger triggers intense cravings for sugar, so when hunger pangs strike, nibble on some protein foods or nuts.

- **Eat plenty of fresh fruits and vegetables.** Many types of produce are full of antioxidants and phytochemicals that eliminate free radicals created by stress.

- **Avoid burnt, barbecued, and fried foods.** These foods burden your body with excessive amounts of damaging free radicals.

- **Eat small, frequent meals instead of a few large ones.** Doing so will help you maintain steady blood sugar levels.

- **Drink two or three cups of green tea daily.** Among its many health benefits green teas have theanine, a unique amino acid that tranquilizes the brain and helps to control cortisol levels.

- **Turn off the TV.** TV exposes you to endless numbers of food commercials that are designed to trigger cravings. Decrease the amount of TV you watch, or if you can't, use the mute button to turn off the sound and walk out of the room during commercials.

- **Eat foods with antistress vitamins and minerals daily.** Make sure to include the B complex and vitamins A, C, and E as well as potassium, magnesium, calcium, and zinc to replenish nutrients depleted by daily stresses.

- **Get enough sleep.** Fatigue and sleep deprivation lead to carb cravings because carbs are a major source of energy needed when you feel wiped out. Instead, to relax before bedtime, eat a dairy food such as yogurt or steamed milk with some honey and cinnamon. Calcium is a natural tranquilizer, muscle relaxant, and sleep promoter.

- **Exercise regularly.** Exercise counteracts stress by releasing endorphins, the exercise hormone that produces good feelings.

- **Consider using herbs.** Passionflower, a traditional Native American herb used to soothe the nerves, contains flavonoids that are natural sedatives promoting calmness and ability to sleep. Passionflower, chamomile, and sassafras teas calm jumpy nerves. (Talk with an herbalist or naturopathic physician for recommendations.)

- **Drink a lot of water.** Every system of the body depends on water to remove wastes, bring nutrients and oxygen to the cells, aid in digestion, and maintain normal metabolic rates. Most adults need about ten cups daily, at least half in the form of plain, clean water.

Spiritual Nourishment

In her book *French Women Don't Get Fat: The Secret of Eating for Pleasure*, Mireille Guilliano, the CEO of a French champagne company, explains why she believes Americans struggle more with their weight than the French. Once when walking through Chicago's O'Hare International Airport, she looked around at people eating and tried to find some who seemed to be enjoying their food. What she found were people gulping down hamburgers and fries while typing on their laptops, talking on cell phones, and reading papers. "I didn't see anyone eating with pleasure. Food is one of the best pleasures in life. We should not eat like we're robots on autopilot. It's not eating, it's stuffing yourself."

Mireille Guilliano's advice to Americans is, "Eat only good food and relax and savor every bite." French women eat with all five of their senses, she explains. "Even when we go to a sandwich shop on the run, we sit down, take our time, look at the sandwich, admire the bread or the butter on it, and eat slowly. We chew well, and we stop between bites."

French women don't have the weight problems of American women. Only 11 percent of French women are obese, compared with one out of three in the United States. Puzzled scientists call it "the French paradox," and many nutritionists have tried to understand the difference. Perhaps Guilliano has found the answer.

The French, she writes, eat real foods, not faux foods, including plenty of fresh vegetables and fruit, but despite the fact that they drink wine at every meal, eat rich sauces, red meat, butter, cheese, and good French bread, they stay slim because they value quality over quantity.

"People in the U.S. would buy a five-pound burrito if it cost 99 cents. French people would never do that," says Guilliano, whose figure is maintained by following the advice of her family physician, given to her after her return from studying in the United States as an exchange student and gaining twenty pounds. His advice was, "Consume three good meals a day, watch portions, eat lots of fruits and vegetables, use seasonings, eat a variety of seasonal foods, drink plenty of water, savor wine, walk, including up and down the stairs, and indulge in a treat once in a while."

At the end of the day, says Guilliano, we have only one body and we need to respect it. We need to know what we are putting into our body and make sure it is doing us some good. If you agree that food should be something more than feed, that it should nourish and delight as well as sustain us, try this little experiment.

For one week, each time you are about to eat, take ten seconds to intentionally and consciously feel heartfelt gratitude for the food you are about to eat. By allowing your heart and mind to center on the food that is about to become part of you, you can turn eating into a transformative experience.

Food is more than something to eat. At its most basic level, it is chemical energy, and it retains some of the characteristics of the living plants and animals from which it came. Does it also retain some of the emotional energy infused into it by the cook? There is no hard-and-fast evidence for this, but haven't you sensed the difference between meals that were thrown together without care and those lovingly prepared and served?

We have been programmed to think of food as units of nutrition that are roughly equivalent. But our minds and bodies respond differently. We feel a certain way after eating a meat meal and another way after eating one made with fish or just vegetables, and our bodies respond in different ways to the chemical and energy characteristics of these meals.

After your moment of gratitude, consider what kind of energy your food contains: does it seem light, stringy, stolid and thick, bouncy? After you do this a few times, you will get better at describing it.

As in the harvest rituals of the first Americans, the intention is to recognize and celebrate the life-sustaining forces in food and eliminate life-diminishing ones. Harvest rituals begin and end with prayers of heartfelt appreciation for the plant and animal foods we are about to eat and the nourishment they provide. Bring this new food awareness to all of your food-related activities. By doing so you will enhance your ability to sense when food is serving your needs and when it is not.

The Vietnamese Buddhist monk, teacher, and peace activist Thich Nhat Hanh offers a Zen blessing said before eating:

> *In this plate of food*
> *I see the entire universe*
> *Supporting my existence.*

It reflects the Buddhist belief that in the simple act of blessing food before eating, we connect with all life and life sources in the universe: plants, animals, people, the elements of sunlight, air, water, and earth. Without this interdependent network, which Thich Nhat Hanh calls "interbeing," there would be no food or life to enjoy. This recognition is where spiritual nourishment begins—and where we begin to eat from the heart, not just for the heart.

Spiritual food wisdom is found in almost all ancient cultures and mystical traditions. Through a heartfelt feeling of gratitude and appreciation of food, we are drawn into a deeper mystical connection with it and the universe. Being grateful for food, you feel compassion for the plants and animals that have become your food and a compassionate connection to the entire food chain that contributes to your nourishment. Each time you eat gratefully you are setting aside your self-focus for a direct experience with something other than your physical self—your food, other people, your surroundings, and your feelings. This transformative experience not only will make you feel good, but it also will make you less prone to heart disease, and possibly, other chronic illnesses.

Research conducted by the Heart–Math Institute of Boulder, Colorado, suggests that the human body consists of both physical and bioenergetic dimensions and that we each have an individual spirit, which is nonphysical in the classical sense, yet has very real, dynamic effects on us.

Further, this research shows that the heart produces the most powerful rhythmic electromagnetic field in the body. The brain and all the cells in the body are continuously bathed in the heart's electromagnetic field. The heart is a carrier of emotional information and a mediator of bioelectromagnetic communication both within and outside the body. Research demonstrates that our heart's energy field changes distinctly as we experience different emotions, and it can register these emotions on the brains and hearts of people around us and even affect cells, water, and DNA in vitro.

Dr. Masaru Emoto, a physician from Japan, studied the affects of prayer and consciousness on the crystal structure of water molecules. He demonstrated that human thoughts and emotions can alter the molecular structure of water. When water was imprinted by thoughts of love, gratitude, and appreciation, it responded by the development of complex beautiful crystalline patterns, and when water was imbued with negative intentions it became disordered and lost its magnificent patterning, taking on grotesque forms. His work, now replicated by others, suggests that thoughts can change our external world as well as our inner one.

From a health point of view, Heart-Math studies indicate that prayer and feelings of gratitude can lower stress hormone levels, raise levels of DHEA, the antiaging hormone, and improve heart rates. The bottom line is that your health will benefit from focusing on your food with gratitude, prayers, or blessings, and your heart will share those feelings with others. Not only will you imbue your nourishment with a deeper spiritual meaning, gratefulness may infuse your heart with positive healing energy that can be communicated to all the cells in your body.

Even when time is short or when you find yourself eating in the car on your way to an appointment, a quick prayer of thanks can be as simple as, "Thank you for this food." Make up your own gratitude statement or borrow one from a faith tradition—Buddhist, Vedic, Muslim, Christian, or Jewish—and think appreciative thoughts as you munch.

In Chapter 8, we will explore some of the underlying causes and nutritional approaches for healing digestive diseases and fibromyalgia.

Healing Digestive Disorders

The destiny of nations depends on how they nourish themselves.

—JEAN ANTHELME BRILLAT-SAVARIN (1825)

My mother had what she called a nervous stomach, and her mother had it, too. What I understood from the term was that mother's GI tract was highly reactive to stress. Anytime there was a family "situation," mother would run off to the bathroom. I didn't think much about it until I was settled into my own marriage with two children and a job that kept me constantly on the go and on edge.

My inherited "nervous stomach" showed up every time I had to make an important presentation, negotiate a contract, or win approval for a project. The problem was annoying but manageable. Fifteen years later, with both my job and marriage in trouble, I found myself in a health crisis for the first time in my life. Suddenly, I was exhausted all the time, barely able to climb the short flight of stairs to the bedroom in my condo; with the smallest exertion my breathing was labored. I experienced bouts of foggy-headedness and gained a ton of weight although I didn't think my diet had changed except that I was eating less. Chest pains, while batting around a tennis ball with a friend, finally got my attention.

It took four M.D.s and me to figure out what was wrong. I remembered something I had read by Abram Hoffer, M.D., Ph.D., the father of orthomolecular medicine, "If the patient has been to more than four physicians, nutrition is probably the medical answer." A physician friend recommended a brilliant diagnostician who was able to pinpoint the problem with my help. It seems I was a classic case of adrenal burnout, with a nonfunctioning thyroid gland and a body in underdrive. I was advised that my recovery could take several years because replacing missing hormones had to be done slowly or I could suffer a massive heart attack. I was only fifty-two years old, too young for life to be slipping away.

Unprepared to deal with my hormonal wipeout, I read everything I could find in the research literature and began the slow, uneven, often depressing process of recovering. I was unable to do the work I was trained for or even maintain relationships I valued. It was only with the greatest effort focused on healing myself (and believing I could) that I was able to come back to life, physically, emotionally, and to my surprise, spiritually.

Oddly, it was only after my health crisis subsided that I was able to identify another health problem—irritable bowel syndrome (IBS), a chronic condition that seemed to be getting worse as my other symptoms subsided. I was forced to acknowledge the problem when my physical reaction to a routine colonoscopy examination was nothing short of explosive! Embarrassed, I hid the problem from everyone I knew, planning my life around frequent, strategic bathroom stops and "emergency repairs."

I couldn't eat wheat, corn, dairy, or three-course meals in restaurants without bloating, discomfort, gassiness, and diarrhea. I started tracking my symptoms. Proteins and vegetables were the least troublesome and starches and some fruits the most. Processed foods caused more discomfort than fresh, organic ones, but anxiety and stress always made my symptoms worse, regardless of what I ate.

IBS: Widespread But Little Known

I didn't know it, but my situation was not unique. One in five children—more girls than boys—who report a history of abdominal pain before age eleven are two to three times more likely to experience IBS as an adult, according to a study in the September 2005 issue of the *American Journal of Gastroenterology*.

IBS is a functional disorder of the large intestine (colon). Instead of contracting and expanding rhythmically to move food along, in IBS, the colon is "irritable;" it makes longer and stronger contractions, accompanied by cramping, abdominal pain, bloating, gas, and changes in bowel habits.

Despite the mystery about what causes it, IBS is second only to the common cold in the number of sick days it generates each year in the United States. In fact, it is the most common gastrointestinal complaint in North America, affecting 20 percent of adults, most of whom are not diagnosed or treated. Although the cause of IBS is unknown, the result is malfunctioning nervous system control over the gut. Stress, menstruation, overeating, certain trigger foods, and food additives prompt flare-ups and make symptoms worse.

Diagnosing IBS

Clinically, a physician looks for several of these symptoms before making a diagnosis of IBS:

- Stool urgency
- Abdominal fullness, distention, or cramping relieved by defecation
- Abnormal bowel function (diarrhea, constipation)
- Secretion of mucus from the colon
- Dyspeptic symptoms (flatulence, belching, nausea, anorexia)
- Anxiety or depression

Criteria for diagnosis have evolved over the last three decades, with the most recent set published in 1992 and refined in 2003. To be diagnosed with IBS, a patient must report twelve or more weeks of abdominal discomfort or pain with two out of three of these additional signs: discomfort relieved by defecation; onset associated with a change in defecation habits (more than three times a day or less than three times per week); change in the form or appearance of stool (lumpy/hard or loose/watery).

Once the criteria are satisfied, a physician must rule out other possible causes, such as infections, malabsorption syndrome, ulcerative colitis, Crohn's disease, diabetes, thyroid disorders, or eating habits. For example, consumption of artificial sweeteners causes diarrhea, and a diet low in fiber and fluids can prompt constipation. Although symptoms may look like IBS at first, if withdrawing sweeteners from the diet restores colon health, IBS is ruled out. Colon cancer is another possibility that must be ruled out by a colonoscopy exam. Although associated with severe pain and discomfort, IBS does not usually lead to cancer or other life-threatening diseases.

Today 54 million Americans, three times more women than men, suffer from IBS. For years the condition was thought to be psychological, as reflected in the names by which it's been known over the years: nervous indigestion, spastic colon, and intestinal neurosis. According to the National Institutes of Health, people with IBS are more sensitive and reactive than other people, and things that don't bother most people can be distressing to them. Studies suggest that this hypersensitivity may be the result of having more pain receptors in the GI tract. Animal studies have shown that gas in the bowel can stretch the bowel wall and cause increased sensitization of receptors in the gut, lowering the threshold for pain. Women experience pain flare-ups around the time of their menstrual periods, leading to unnecessary hysterectomies when IBS is mistaken for chronic pelvic pain. If IBS is the cause of the pain, a hysterectomy doesn't eliminate the problem.

Conventional Treatment

GI infections and inflammation cause changes in the cells of the gut that persist after the infections and inflammations resolve. Psychosocial stresses, such as anxiety and depression, also can cause changes in the colon. The gut-brain connection in IBS is a basis for several drug treatments designed to block serotonin reuptake in the gut, in the same way serotonin reuptake inhibitors (SSRIs) are used to treat psychiatric disorders.

Most of the serotonin in the body (95 percent) is made in the GI tract, where it is involved in gut motility and sensitivity as well as in influencing moods. One IBS drug, Alosetron (Lotronex) was taken off the market in 2000 after reports of severe complications and at least four deaths among users. The FDA now allows Alosetron to be prescribed medically with some restrictions.

Conventional drug treatments for IBS include:

- Drugs designed to relax intestinal muscle to relieve cramping associated with muscle spasms (Bentyl, Levsin, Levsinex)
- Antidepressants for depression and anxiety (SSRIs such as Prozac, Paxil)
- Antidiarrheal agents for stopping diarrhea (Lomotil, Imodium)
- Bulk-forming laxatives and fiber for constipation (Metamucil, guar gum)
- SSRIs for short-term treatment of constipation
- Tegaserod maleate (Zelnorm) and Alosetron HCL (Lotronex) for patients with frequent and severe abdominal discomfort and bowel urgency

None of these prescriptive drugs are panaceas and the SSRIs, in particular, have frequent and severe—potentially life-threatening—side effects. Many patients with

IBS are disillusioned by the lack of effective treatments for their debilitating, persistent symptoms and seek help from alternative medicine, although some alternative approaches are questioned as well.

Alternative Approaches to Treating IBS

Carolyn Dean, M.D., N.D., a Canadian medical and naturopathic doctor, herbalist, acupuncturist, and nutritionist, and the author of *Irritable Bowel for Dummies* (John Wiley & Sons, October 2005) and a dozen other books, says that although no single cause of IBS has been found, its onset is often preceded by an infection. Given the extremely high rate of food-borne intestinal illness in North America, intestinal infection could be a plausible explanation for the high prevalence of IBS.

The Centers for Disease Control (CDC) estimates that each year 76 million people get sick, more than three hundred thousand are hospitalized, and five thousand die as a result of infectious material in foods causing illness, especially among the young, elderly, and immune-compromised. The CDC expects these problems to grow worse in the years ahead because of changes in human demographics, food preferences, food production and distribution, microbial adaptation, and lack of support for public health that have led to the emergence of novel diseases as well as traditional ones. With increasing travel, the risk of contracting and spreading a food-borne illness now exists at the local, regional, and even global levels.

After a bout of intestinal infection, says Dean, many people can no longer digest wheat and dairy foods and are prone to overgrowth of candida (yeast), a side effect of antibiotic treatment that wipes out the colon's normal colony of bacteria. Susceptible people don't seem to get over these GI problems, says Dean, but things get worse when they experience stress or go on weight loss diets. Ultimately, they develop an overgrowth of candida, "leaky gut" syndrome, gluten intolerance to wheat, rye, oats, and barley, among other food sensitivities, have gassy and burpy reactions to sulfur-containing foods (cabbage, onion, garlic, egg yolk, and sulfur-containing food additives and medicines), and intolerance to fruit sugars and high fructose sweeteners.

Here is a definition of a condition called *Crook's candidiasis*, made available by Dr. Dean, that differs from the conventional medical definition of yeast infection, which is limited to a skin and mucus membrane infection of the mouth or vagina or a blood infection. Crook's candidiasis describes a different condition. It encompasses:

- Overgrowth of yeast in the intestines that changes under the influence of antibiotics, birth control pills, cortisone, and a high refined sugar diet into a tissue invasive form that causes intestinal inflammation and leaky gut syndrome as well as symptoms of IBS

- Yeast overgrowth that presents as allergy with burning and itching of various parts of the body, including nasal membranes, sinuses, skin, and vagina

- Multiple and sometimes severe reactions in the body to the 180 different byproducts and wastes from yeast

Sugars from milk, fruit, and honey as well as refined sugars and industrial sweeteners in commercial foods and drinks feed overgrowth of candida in the colon, setting up a vicious cycle. Some food factors make matters worse. The artificial sweetener aspartame directly triggers IBS, and sorbitol, a sweetener that is only partially absorbed in the body, also irritates the bowel. Fatty foods also may trigger IBS. Dietary fat stimulates bile production, which can make diarrhea worse for IBS sufferers. For that reason a low- or moderately low-fat diet is recommended.

Although IBS is not a classic inflammatory disease, there is evidence that microscopic inflammatory complexes are present, which can and probably do develop into full-blown inflammatory colitis or Crohn's disease if the patient's "inflammatory behaviors" are not changed, says Dean. Eating a proper diet low in inflammatory factors is the key to managing IBS symptoms.

Dr. Andrew Weil suggests keeping a symptom diary to pinpoint flare-ups and foods that cause distress. Common trigger foods are coffee, gluten, dairy products, fatty foods, fructose (and high fructose corn syrup), and non-nutritive sweeteners used in "sugar free" foods and gums. Also helpful are eating smaller, more frequent meals and a fiber-rich diet such as that advised in Chapter 2's "Ten Rules for Healthy Eating." If you experience more gassiness and bloating as a result of eating more fiber-rich foods, be patient, Weil advises. The diet will help to prevent cramping and soften tools, and you will experience less bloating and gas as your body adjusts to foods with higher fiber levels.

Several dietary supplements have proven to be helpful for IBS. You can buy these over-the-counter at a health food store or from your natural pharmacist. Follow usage directions on the package or bottle.

- **Peppermint oil.** It relaxes the smooth muscle of the GI tract, reducing cramping, bloating, and stool frequency. Dr. Weil recommends two enteric-coated capsules three times a day between meals.

- **Probiotic supplements.** These counteract unfriendly microorganisms such as candida, relieve symptoms, and can bring about a remission in IBS. Research from University College Cork (www.ucc.ie/en/) in Ireland found that patients who consumed probiotic supplements (Bifidabacterium infantis 35624) daily for eight weeks experienced fewer overall symptoms of IBS and less abdominal pain.

- **Marshmallow root.** This herb helps to coat and soothe inflamed tissues in the gut. It can be taken as a tincture or in capsules.

Natural Treatment Protocols

A three-step strategy for people with IBS is recommended. The first step is to get your symptoms under control. The following interventions have proven effective with one or more of the associated symptoms of IBS.

- Controlling candida overgrowth, which produces more than one hundred-eighty toxic and allergy-triggering byproducts that cause inflammation of the intestinal walls; uncontrolled it can result in IBS and fibromyalgia, negatively affecting absorption of nutrients and causing gas, belching, bloating, and pain after meals

- Avoiding the fifty thousand largely untested chemicals used in commercial food production, all of which can trigger negative reactions in the body

- Using organic tinctures to get rid of toxic viruses and bacteria that continue to colonize in our bodies long after they have run their courses as acute illnesses

- Taking digestive enzymes before the beginning of a meal to lessen excessive gassiness and bloating caused by too few beneficial bacteria that make some of the digestive enzymes needed in the bowel

- Consuming enough soluble fiber and nutrients from fruits and vegetables to enhance bile flow and improve the transit time of food passing through the colon

- Making lifestyle changes to reduce stress and depression: massage, meditation, moderate exercise such as walking, listening to calming music, hypnotherapy, and acupuncture

Step two is to revamp your diet. Dietary approaches depend on your symptoms. For people with yeast overgrowth, a candida diet is recommended, including avoiding sugary and starchy foods and foods that contain yeast. A self-test for the relationship of yeast to IBS symptoms, as well as sensitivity to other foods, is outlined in the next section.

If you have IBS and don't plan to test for yeast or have completed testing and treatment, Dr. Dean suggests making the following eating changes and sticking with them for at least three weeks.

- Eat a high-fiber diet with primarily soluble fiber, including fruits, vegetables, whole grains, and beans; avoid insoluble fiber foods including wheat kernels, popcorn, apple skins, and nuts
- Avoid sugars (including honey), wheat, and dairy

If you continue to experience symptoms after three weeks, the next step is to follow the dietary recommendations found on the website www.yeastconnections.com, where Dr. Dean is a medical advisor. After several weeks, if your symptoms show little improvement, try the avoidance and challenge protocol described in the next section to identify specific food sensitivities and eliminate them from your diet.

Self-Test for Relationship Between Yeast and IBS Symptoms

A study by Norwegian and British scientists, "Yeast Metabolic Products, Yeast Antigens, and Yeasts as Possible Triggers for Irritable Bowel Syndrome," published in the *European Journal of Gastroenterology* [17, no. 1 (2005): 21–26], suggests a test diet in order to study the cross-reactivity of yeast and IBS symptoms. Included in the article are lists of foods to be avoided, foods to eat, and a procedure for a "provocation self-test" that allows you to determine your allergic sensitivity to specific foods.

There are several types of foods you need to avoid before you start self-testing. These foods include:

- **Sugars.** Malt, honey, maple syrup, sweetened foods, soft drinks, ice cream, cakes, pastries, pies, biscuits, buns, chocolate, sweets, candy, chewing gum, ready-sweetened breakfast cereals, nutrition bars, canned fruits and vegetables, and sweet potatoes

- **Yeast.** Bread, rolls, bread mixes, breadcrumbs, bread pudding, bread stuffing, tortillas, sourdough, beer, brewer's yeast, soy sauce, pickles, cough syrup, alcoholic beverages, and nutritional supplements containing yeast

- **Mold proteins.** Soy margarines and oils, vinegar, mustard, dressing, ketchup, pickles, relishes, smoked meats, smoked fish, mushrooms, cheese, unrefrigerated orange juice, leftovers, and citric acid

- **Milk sugar.** Milk and milk products like yogurt, sour cream, milky sweets, and lactose (as an ingredient in prepared foods and pills)

- **Medications.** Discontinue antibiotics, prednisone, and antihistamines (allergy tablets) at least five days prior to starting the following elimination diet—in order to be able to recognize allergic reactions to individual foods

- Eliminate any foods that you know you don't tolerate well

The following foods are recommended as your basic diet before starting the testing procedure. Follow this diet for a minimum of nine days before you start testing foods to add to your diet.

- Meat, fish, eggs, chicken (not marinated)
- All vegetables (fresh and frozen), potatoes, sprouts (not moldy)
- Rice, grain, flour, pasta
- Fruits (fresh or frozen), which have been washed and peeled, maximum about ½ pound daily; avoid grapes, plums, overripe fruit such as bananas with brown spots, and soft pears, which contain a lot of fructose
- Soda bread, crisp bread without yeast and malt, rice cakes
- Butter, margarine without soy oil
- Nuts and seeds
- Small amount of milk in bread or cream cheese; soy milk, rice milk
- Freshly squeezed juice, sparkling water, mold-free herbal tea, a few cups of black tea or coffee

After you have followed the basic diet for at least nine days, you are ready to begin the avoidance and challenge protocol for identifying food sensitivities. Eat the test foods at breakfast. Add each test ingredient one at a time on the day indicated:

- **Day 1.** ¼ teaspoon vinegar in a glass of water or on a salad
- **Day 2.** Yeast from beer (¼ cup beer) or 1 brewer's yeast tablet
- **Day 3.** ¼ pint milk or sour cream
- **Day 4.** 1 slice ordinary bread (with yeast)
- **Day 5.** 1 ounce sugar, honey, or chocolate

If you have an itch or other sensitivity reaction after introducing a food or ingredient, postpone testing other foods until the reaction is gone. If you have a reaction on Day 1, 2, or 4 within twenty-four hours, you probably have a cross allergy to yeast. If you react to milk, you may have a milk sugar (or lactose) intolerance. If you are not quite sure if you have a reaction to a food, wait four days and test again. Sugars are tested last because reactions can be delayed for up to three days.

Food products that you react to should be avoided for two to three months while you take an antifungal medication and probiotic (acidophilus and bifidobacter) before trying them again. It's a good idea to seek the help of a qualified holistic practitioner who can determine if there are other causes for your reactivity, including chemical sensitivities, mercury toxicity, or gluten intolerance.

A Physician's Tale

Judith Petry, M.D., director of Vermont Healing Tools, retired from her busy plastic surgery practice in Boston and moved to a farm in rural Vermont. The move to the country was a huge life change, accompanied with unmanageable bleeding from a uterine fibroid. Dr. Petry's gynecologist advised a hysterectomy, but Dr. Petry didn't want to undergo surgery. Instead, she sought out a naturopathic physician who helped her to manage her hormonal imbalance with a whole foods diet. When she started eating whole grains, however, she started having problems with diarrhea, depression, and headaches from hidden food allergies that flared up now that she was eating a natural, unadulterated diet. She went on an elimination diet, similar to the one described in this chapter. After two weeks on a wheat-free diet, she says, she thought she was going to die because she missed wheat products so much. Finally, she discovered bread made out of almond flour, and that saved the day.

Other grains were tested and she discovered a serious allergy to brown rice. Petry's symptoms were depression, joint pains, headaches, and belly pain. It made her wonder how much of the depression, emotional imbalance, and joint pain that physicians see are caused by food allergies? Probably a lot, she concludes, because some foods don't harmonize with our bodies. As she thought about it, she realized that emotional imbalance can come from food imbalance. She wondered if the addictive way we are accustomed to eating reflects an imbalance in our relationship with the planet, a damaged interface with our external environment that is reflected in inflammation and pain in our internal environment.

"Food is all about the creation of energy," says Petry, "We need to ask ourselves, what kind of energy do we want to create? We're asleep. How do we wake up?" Answering her own question, she told me, "We need to create a new reality. We're talking about vibrating at a different frequency and waking up to see possibilities we couldn't see at the lower frequency. There are solutions available to us that are not yet revealed. It's as if we are seeing everything in beta when we could be seeing it in alpha."

I asked her how we could change our perceptions to see these new solutions to our problems? She answered, "Through prayer and meditation, which connects you with a different frequency. By prayer I don't mean asking someone for something, but connecting and feeling the continuity of all things."

The following certified organic foods Dr. Petry now eats with pleasure and without pain, every day:

- Fried eggs in olive oil
- Gluten-free bread from bean and potato flour
- Nuts such as pumpkin seeds, walnuts, pecans
- Field salad
- Fish such as salmon, scallops, tuna
- Zucchini, mushrooms, broccoli, carrots, parsnips, chard
- Beans such as kidney and red lentils
- Quinoa—a grain
- Vegetable stews
- Beef—once a week
- Yogurt with fruit
- Grapes

Petry offers this advice, "If you have to give up bread, expect to grieve for its loss. Allow yourself to experience grieving and recognize that another door is opening. I still miss pizza, but like my dead grandmother whom I miss, I'm not going to bring it back in this lifetime."

When asked how these ideas fit within the medical model in which she was trained, Petry replied, "I have come to see that when your ability to absorb food is impaired, it represents a damaged interface with the environment. To heal, we need to be conscious of what we are putting into our bodies and into the earth. We are missing the relationship between the earth and our bodies. We are separated from the earth, and like a grieving child who has lost a parent, we are depressed and angry about it."

Our digestive system, which is a part of our nervous system, is asking us to look at what is going on in our lives, says Petry. When we don't listen, we get into patterns of gut damage because anxiety is manifest immediately in our GI tracts.

Fibromyalgia, Chronic Fatigue, and Hypothyroidism

Fibromyalgia (FM) is a pain syndrome that affects the muscles and soft tissues. It occurs in about 4 percent of the population, mainly in women twenty to fifty years of age. People who suffer from it report aching pain, tenderness, and stiffness of the muscles and tendons where they attach to bone. Affected areas tend to be around the base of the skull, the neck, shoulders, thorax, low back, and thighs, and each of the areas can have trigger points that are especially sensitive. FM is one of the most deceptive conditions seen in doctors' offices because symptoms overlap with those of several other disorders.

Symptoms of FM, which include depression, anxiety, and poor sleep, can be confused with those of chronic fatigue syndrome (CFS). For some, the condition is severe enough to be disabling, but others are only mildly uncomfortable. CFS and FM share another trait; there are few remedies. Dr. Dean believes the two conditions are close cousins.

Only recognized medically since 1988, CFS, now known as chronic fatigue and immune dysfunction syndrome or CFIDS, is characterized by extreme fatigue, muscle and joint aches and pains, muscle weakness, chronic headaches, swollen glands, periodic fever and chills, sore throat, numbness and tingling in extremities, inability to cope with stress, cognitive dysfunction, and insomnia. Patients with CFIDS, FM, and yeast overgrowth all complain of being "so tired" and sick all over, and find relief following antiyeast diets and other protocols for controlling yeast overgrowth. But conventional medicine does not recognize the yeast problem or routinely treat FM patients for yeast overgrowth.

It wasn't until 1990 that the American College of Rheumatology established diagnostic criteria for FM, which include incapacitating fatigue, muscle and joint pain, neuralgia, sleep disorders, anxiety, depression, cognitive confusion, and digestive problems. Although there hasn't been much interest in the conventional medical establishment in studying how yeast affects people with either of these disorders, one recent report of one thousand CFIDS patients who were given antifungal medication for yeast found that up to 75 percent of them had yeast overgrowth.

There is no established cause of FM, but physical and emotional stress brings it out. People who have the condition often have lower than normal levels of serotonin, which could explain their sleep difficulties and why the severity of pain differs so widely among patients. There is a great deal of scientific speculation about what causes FM, including physical and mental stress, poor sleep, trauma, exposure to dampness or cold, environmental stress, a viral disorder such as Epstein-Barr virus (EBV), or a bacterial infection like Lyme disease. The disorder can go into remission spontaneously when stress is decreased, but it also may recur at frequent intervals. Dr. Dean, who has written about this, recommends self-help methods that include stretching exercises, relaxation therapy, techniques and supplements to improve sleep, and local applications of heat and gentle massage, as well as counseling.

FM and Hypothyroidism

A question puzzling health practitioners concerned with FM are muscle and joint pain that occurs with hypothyroidism (an underactive thyroid). Are they separate problems or symptoms of thyroid disease? Many patients who are on thyroid replacement medications find that over time they develop more and more joint and muscle pain and arthritislike symptoms. Some doctors believe that patients develop FM and dysfunctional thyroid independently. But what really may be happening is that the pain and achiness are indications of an undertreated thyroid.

Some practitioners speculate that FM is a symptom of an underactive thyroid gland, not necessarily an independent disease. Dr. John C. Lowe, director of research for the Fibromyalgia Research Foundation, thinks so: "In some patients, inadequate tissue regulation by thyroid hormone is the result of cellular resistance to thyroid hormone. In other people, inadequate regulation is the result of a thyroid hormone deficiency."

When Dr. Lowe talks about FM, he means a set of symptoms and signs caused by either too little thyroid hormone produced by the thyroid gland or cellular resistance to the form of the hormone produced by the gland. But because conventional medicine's view is that the only cause of thyroid deficiency is hypothyroidism—a short-age in the amount of hormone produced—many patients are un- or undertreated and develop symptoms of FM, which are all symptoms of inadequate thyroid hormone regulation, according to Dr. Lowe.

People often develop FM after a traumatic event, but they were probably hypothyroid before the trauma. Trauma patients are often physically inactive for some time after their trauma and lose muscle mass from inac-tivity, which further lowers their metabolic rate and leads to the development of FM, probably made worse by the typical American diet and failure to take nutritional supplements. The three factors, hypothyroidism, nutri-tional insufficiencies, and inadequate physical activity combine to lower metabolism and create obesity.

When Dr. Lowe starts working with these patients, he attempts to improve their FM first, and urges them to be patient because it can take up to four months to see sig-nificant results and feel better. Dr. Lowe believes that the best qualified practitioners to work with FM patients are naturopaths. "I am referring to those who graduated from accredited naturopathic medical schools and are eligible to be licensed in states that license naturopathic physicians." He says that these physicians are far more willing to do the medical detective work that conventional physicians have abandoned.

CFIDS

The CFIDS Association estimates that eight hundred thousand Americans have CFIDS, with 90 percent of them undiagnosed. CFIDS is about three times more common in women than men, a rate similar to that for other autoimmune diseases such as multiple sclerosis and lupus. CFIDS is four times more common than HIV infections in women, and more likely to show up in a woman's life than lung cancer. Once called "yuppie flu," it is now recognized in every ethnic and income segment, and causes remain unknown.

Symptoms of CFIDS, in addition to muscle pain, include multijoint pain without swelling or redness, lack of refreshing sleep, incapacitating fatigue lasting more than twenty-four hours after exercise, profound exhaustion, extremely poor stamina, impaired short-term memory and concentration, sore throat, tender lymph nodes, and severe headaches.

For years, CFIDS patients were told, "It is all in your head," that they had a psychological disorder treatable with drugs and talk therapy. Because many people with CFIDS are extremely sensitive to drug therapy, they find most relief from natural nutrients and noninvasive therapies.

Some of these treatments used by Dr. Dean include:

- Supplements for digestive problems and nausea, including probiotics, digestive enzymes, and ginger
- Supplements for depression and anxiety, including St. John's wort, tryptophan, and 5-HTP
- Supplements for muscle and joint pain, including magnesium malate and glucosamine sulphate
- Counseling to develop the coping skills necessary to live with a debilitating chronic illness

- Gentle yoga
- Sleep and rest management

Speculations About Origins of CFS and FM

In the 1980s, Dr. Dean began treating a number of patients with chronic fatigue syndrome. They presented with chronic yeast overgrowth in their bodies from antibiotics and high-sugar diets. After that came a wave of patients with FM. As Dr. Dean treated these cases, she began to feel that these two conditions might be different manifestations of just one—ongoing poisoning of the body.

The women she treated ate diets high in bread and sugar, took birth control pills, antihistamines, antidepressants, and had been treated with antibiotics, all of which, she speculated, could have contributed to an overload of toxins and yeast in their bodies that taxed their immune systems, leaving them vulnerable to infection.

Individuals who are immune-compromised often have chronic sinus, throat, chest, and bladder infections. If they are given more medications to treat those conditions, they can experience even more side effects and develop allergies to all medications. This scenario was repeated countless times in the patients who came to Dr. Dean's clinic throughout the 1980s. But it wasn't until she started studying Chinese medicine that she understood what caused her patients to become vulnerable and how an unbalanced diet was perpetuating the problem.

Chinese medicine is based on the philosophy that food is medicine and medicine is food. After diagnosing your condition, a Chinese doctor works with you to create an eating plan that stresses the foods that will help bring your body back into balance and keep it there. Each type of food, from fruits and vegetables to meat, fish, herbs, and spices, has its own specific quality and action on the body and makes a unique contribution to restoring the body's natural state of balance and harmony.

A number of illnesses have a spectrum of symptoms similar to that of CFIDS. These include FM, myalgic encephalomyelitis, neurasthenia, multiple chemical sensitivities, and chronic mononucleosis. Although these illnesses may present with a primary symptom other than fatigue, chronic fatigue is commonly associated with all of them. Perhaps the human toll of these disorders will help us come to a greater understanding of nutrition and its importance to our physical and mental well-being.

For More Information

For more information about digestive disorders, visit these websites:

- American College of Gastroenterology (acg.gi.org)
- Irritable Bowel Syndrome Self-Help Group (ibsgroup .org)
- International Foundation for Functional Gastrointestinal Disorders (iffgd.org)
- The Cleveland Clinic Foundation (clevelandclinic .org)

- The National Digestive Diseases Information Clearinghouse (niddk.nih.gov/health/digest/nddic.htm)
- The Centers for Disease Control (cdc.gov/ncidod/diseases/cfs/about/what.htm).

To find alternative medical practitioners, visit these websites:

- American Association of Naturopathic Physicians (naturopathic.org)
- American Holistic Medical Association (holistic medicine.org)
- American Chinese Medicine Association (american chinesemedicineassociation.org)

In Chapter 9, we will evaluate popular weight reduction diets in terms of their ability to support nutritional balance and healthy eating. In order to lose weight, we shouldn't have to compromise our health.

Slimming Without Tears

Researchers in Boston found that when obese people consumed as many carbohydrates with a low-glycemic index as they wanted, they lost just as much weight in twelve months as people who stuck with a conventional calorie-restricted, low-fat diet.

—Dr. David S. Ludwig (May 2005)

For years we've been told that it's all about the calories—calories in and calories out. The latest weight loss advice from the federal government says that, and so do most of the weight loss experts we hear on TV. No matter what the experts tell us or how appealing a calorie-controlled plan may seem, for many of us the advice is disastrous. You'll probably lose weight for the first few weeks or months on any calorie-restricted plan, but when the weight loss tapers off or stalls, as it inevitably will, you'll become discouraged and abandon what you've worked so hard to accomplish.

"Dieting is counterproductive," says Dr. Linda Bacon of the University of California at Davis, lead researcher of a two-year study of obese women who were chronic dieters. The study compared women following a calorie-restricted diet and exercise program with women focused on a healthy lifestyle and self-acceptance but not weight loss. Women on the diet and exercise program regained more weight than they initially lost and didn't sustain improvements in their cholesterol and blood pressure levels, while the women who weren't counting calories did have long-term improvements in these health indices.

If you've regained the weight you lost dieting, you will probably try another diet, but if you join the ranks of yo-yo dieters, your weight problems are going to grow more intractable. Dr. Bacon believes that overweight people would do better to embrace exercise as a way to improve their health and feel better, rather than low-calorie, low-fat, or low-carb diets. Her advice is, "Stop dieting and start listening to your body's hunger signals before deciding when and what to eat." Most people are not tuned in to their bodies, says Dr. Bacon.

A Lose-Lose Situation

What we believe about weight loss and how our bodies work are two different things. Most of us who are weight challenged have bought into the fable that we can have fast and easy weight loss by cutting down on what and how much we eat. We want to try every new diet plan that hits the airwaves because we desperately are looking for the secret of effortless weight loss that we've been promised is out there. If we just eat fewer carbohydrates, more fats, more meat, less fat, more fiber, no grains, whole grains, grapefruit, cabbage soup . . . fill in your own favorite secret, we finally will be able to get our weight under control. Unfortunately, it doesn't work that way.

Yo-yo dieting, the pattern of on-again, off-again restrictive eating, sets us up for getting fatter as we get older. The vicious cycle of weight loss, gain, loss, gain, is called the rebound effect, and it is our body's biological defense against not getting enough to eat. The weight you lose on a "sure-fire diet plan guaranteed to burn off ten pounds in ten days" will probably stay off as long as you remain physically active and in good health, but any trauma, from a sprained ankle to a bout of flu, or just slid- ing back into your old eating habits, can cause you to gain back the weight you've lost and then some more.

Eventually, you'll be tempted to try again, but your next experience is not likely to be any more successful than the last. In fact, if you want to avoid gaining more pounds, you should avoid dieting. Instead of spinning through another diet cycle, you can achieve a healthy weight by following the "Ten Rules for Healthy Eating," based on natural, organic foods in the variety and balance needed for long-term health. By following these guide- lines, a high-fiber, low energy-density approach to meals and snacks, along with a moderate amount of physical activity, you can achieve a slow, steady, long-term weight loss, improve your nutrition, protect yourself against diet- related diseases, and avoid feeling depleted, lethargic, and deprived.

It may sound like a tall order, but it is a reasonable one if your hormones and digestive system are functioning normally. The keys to weight loss success, according to dozens of the latest studies, are eating your fill of foods naturally rich in fiber and nutrients and staying away from concentrated calories—foods and drinks loaded with sweeteners and commercial fats.

You won't lose weight fast, and you may not get down to the size you were when you went to your high school prom, but let's not kid ourselves: weight at age forty or fifty is not usually the same as it was at age seventeen. And you probably won't go from a dress size of 18 to a 3. You can get closer to that shape if you work out in a gym with a personal trainer for three to five hours a day, eat a body-builder's diet, and make the "body beautiful" your obsession, but it doesn't come cheap. Fortunately, it's not what most of us are looking for, and not what I recommend as a nutritionist.

Most of the commercial diet plans promoted in women's magazines and in hot bestsellers are rehashes of old dieting ideas, but dieters are so desperate for the next best thing that even the wildest claims of success have some credibility with us. Avoid them like the plague! All calorie-restricted diets cause your body to rebound by slowing down your metabolism and saving calories for a hypothetical approaching famine. Worse, your old cravings and powerful urges to binge will return with a vengeance as soon as you go off the diet reservation. So why go there?

A psychiatrist I know says dieting is a lot like going without sleep. You can't help but be tired if you don't get enough sleep. You can go without it for a day or two with enough caffeine and pills, but you can't extinguish your body's preprogrammed need for sleep, no matter what you do. In the same way, you can't overcome your preprogrammed need for enough food to sustain your body weight. It's basic physiology.

Conventional calorie-restricted diets don't work because they're counter physiological and they will, eventually, result in your gaining more weight than you lost while dieting. Instead of being trapped in a prison of calorie restriction, why not escape from dieting hell by adopting what our mothers (or grandmothers) used to call good food habits. I don't mean the kind of eating endorsed by certain food trade groups (the milk mustache people, the "beef—it's what's for dinner" folks, or "Betty Crocker"), but whole, fresh foods such as those recommended in this book, based on the types of meals and menus that have supported human health for thousands of years.

If it sounds like everything you thought you knew about weight loss is turning out to be wrong, it probably is. We're in the midst of a profound paradigm shift in the battle of the bulge, says Dr. Bacon. Instead of putting all our efforts on losing excess weight, people should focus on exercising as a way to improve health and feel better, and instead of following strict diet regimens, listen to our body's inner cues for when to eat. The idea of accepting obesity bothers many people, including most physicians, but Bacon's studies and those of other researchers suggest that their concerns are unwarranted.

New Breakthroughs

Researchers in Boston, along with dozens of other research teams, have found that when overweight people ate as many carbohydrates as they desired, as long as they were low glycemic index foods that are digested slowly and cause slow increases in blood sugar, they lost weight permanently and reduced their risk of heart disease. Low glycemic foods are whole, fresh, fiber-rich foods that are minimally processed and low in sugars and fats. They include nonstarchy vegetables, fresh fruit, beans, and peas, 100 percent whole grains, nuts, and dairy products.

Where we get into trouble is when we eat megaportions of highly refined white flour, sugar-rich, calorie-dense, processed foods that have a lot of eye and mouth appeal but negative impacts on our bodies. Our bodies just can't handle these refined, sweetened, and greased foods very well. The proof is apparent on the streets and in the clinics of the United States. With more people getting fatter and sicker at all ages, in all stages of life, and at every income level, we have to recognize that the problem is not just personal but societal, and the remedies must be societal, not just personal. (For a discussion of ideas on this topic, see Chapter 10.)

A novel approach to weight management has come from the laboratory of Professor Barbara Rolls of Penn State University. Some call it a paradigm shift because it is a thoroughly different way of looking at the subject; instead of considering the ratio of fat, carbs, and protein as the key to dieting success, Dr. Rolls has been studying volumetrics. In her studies, people who ate fewer calories but more low energy-density foods (fruits, vegetables, soups, low-fat entrees) lost more weight than dieters who ate more concentrated calorie choices, and people who ate multicourse meals ate more food than people who ate just one dish.

According to Dr. Rolls, the key to weight loss is selecting foods that help you feel full with fewer calories. Most diets don't work very well or very long because they aren't satisfying. "Satiety is the missing factor," says Rolls, who is frustrated by those who tell dieters to eat less. Her research shows that dieters need to eat more low energy-density foods that are high in fiber and water and fewer calorie-dense foods. People who are most successful in losing weight eat the same amount of food as others (about three pounds) but fewer calories.

In the Laboratory for the Study of Human Ingestive Behavior, directed by Dr. Rolls, an international obesity authority, both normal weight and overweight men and women are observed selecting and eating meals and snacks. These observational studies show that both normal weight and overweight people eat the same weight/volume of foods daily. The difference between normal and overweight people is the caloric value of the food they select. This suggests that as long as you eat the same volume of food, just lowering the calorie density of the food will leave you feeling full and satisfied.

Dr. Rolls says you don't have to eliminate any food you like (such as chocolate) because of its energy density. What counts is the overall energy density of what you eat. Instead of choosing the lowest fat foods you can find, choose more foods that are water-filled, like fruits and vegetables, soups and salads, even chocolate milk, which has more water than a chocolate bar.

Another intriguing finding from the lab is that neither normal nor overweight people are able to restrict themselves to a single moderate portion of food if there's extra food on their plates. But it's not just bigger portions that add to our weight woes; it's eating bigger portions of calorie-concentrated foods, like the meals and snacks served in fast-food and chain restaurants. Big portions of lower-calorie food, such as fruits, vegetables, and broth-based soups, can be just as filling and satisfying but deliver fewer calories. What's more, according to the Penn State researchers, a healthy diet can result in significant weight loss without the need to count calories or grams of fat. In other words, forget dieting, just eat healthy!

What about using food labels to find foods with the fewest calories? Studies in the Penn State lab showed that people use food labels to find "low-fat" foods in order to eat bigger portions, in other words, they use the label as a license to eat more.

The reason diets don't work, says Dr. Rolls, is because they're missing the satiety factor. "People need to eat more fruits and vegetables every day so they get satisfying amounts of food and enough calories." Humans eat about the same weight of food daily, says Rolls. So telling people to eat less doesn't work.

"We need to tell people to eat more fruits, veggies, and whole grains, in order to lose weight. In our studies, people who eat more healthy food end up losing more weight than those who cut down on calories. It's the only way to reconcile a big appetite with a small dress size."

Diet Revolutions

In the time it has taken us in North America to become the fattest people on the planet, a truckload of runaway bestsellers have offered us innovative prescriptions for losing weight without losing our minds or our health. The three bestsellers I've chosen to review represent three of the most popular and best-known weight loss diets:

- *Dr. Atkin's Diet Revolution* (1981)
- *Eat More, Weigh Less: Dr. Dean Ornish's Life Choice Program for Losing Weight Safely While Eating Abundantly* (1991)
- Dr. Arthur Agatston's *The South Beach Diet* (2003)

Let's look at how these popular diet approaches stack up against the "Ten Rules for Healthy Eating" in Chapter 2. Until now, most books on dieting have been oblivious to the importance of eating enough food to feel full and satiated while dieting and the importance of low energy-density foods—foods high in fiber and water.

The Atkins Diet

The Atkins diet was the first to recognize the satiety value of a high-protein diet as a boon in following a restricted diet plan. The Atkins diet and other low-carbohydrate diets do help some people lose unwanted weight. But they are not the healthiest diets because they are unbalanced in nutrients and excessive in saturated fats and protein. There is also evidence of dysfunction in the arteries that supply blood to the heart after eating a meal of this type.

In phase 1 of the Atkins diet, the induction phase, you can have unlimited protein, good fats (such as olive oil), and 3 cups of salad and other nonstarchy veggies. Carbohydrates are limited to 20 grams of "net carbs" (carbs minus their fiber). After two weeks, you go on the ongoing weight loss phase (phase 2), which allows the same foods as phase 1, but week by week you add back more carbohydrates: more veggies, cheese, berries, nuts, and seeds. You go from 20 grams of carbs up to 60 grams in 5-gram increments weekly. Phase 3 is premaintenance for the period when you're in sight of your goal. You now add 10 grams of net carbs daily to your diet, or an extra 20 to 30 grams two times weekly. If your weight loss stops, you cut back carbs in 5- to 10-gram blocks until you resume losing.

In phase 4, the lifetime maintenance phase, which begins when you achieve your goal weight, you consume between 60 and 120 grams of net carbs daily, whatever number of carbs you can eat without gaining weight. You stay on this phase for the rest of your life. The minuses of this diet include that it contains unhealthy levels of protein potentially damaging for your kidneys and your metabolic balance; it is missing some of the essential nutrients; and those who follow it tend to eat too few calories because they lose their appetites, resulting in slowed or stopped weight loss.

As soon as you go off this diet and resume "normal eating" you will rebound. A healthier approach would be to eat low glycemic index carbs—whole grains, beans, fruits, vegetables, monounsaturated fats (olive oil, avocado), omega-3 fats (salmon, walnuts, flaxseeds), and a ratio of about 10 to 20 percent protein, 30 percent fat, and 50 to 60 percent low-energy carbs. This type of diet is both filling and satiating, and most people seem able to stick with it long-term, losing weight gradually.

Dr. Ornish's Eat More, Weigh Less

Dr. Dean Ornish, a cardiologist, designed his *Eat More, Weigh Less* plan based on decades of heart research. He was the first to show that you can reverse heart disease by diet alone. In order to reverse blocked arteries, fat levels are dropped to 10 percent of calories, an extremely low level that reduces the palatability and satiety value of this diet. No animal foods, oils, or sugars are allowed in this diet, which is essentially vegetarian.

While the diet is proven to work for recovering heart patients, most people find it difficult to follow because the foods are so limited: tofu, vegetables, beans, fruits, and complex carbs. You can (and will) lose weight on this diet, but most people can't stick to it very long because of its monotony and limited taste appeal. This plan also misses some vitamins and minerals because of its limited range of foods, so you should take a vitamin-mineral supplement when on it.

The South Beach Diet

Dr. Agatston's *The South Beach Diet* tells us the faster sugars and starches are processed and absorbed into your bloodstream, the fatter you get. The South Beach diet is designed to slow down the process of digestion and absorption by combining foods, offering high-fiber foods, and suggesting ways to lower the glycemic index of meals. This diet, designed by another cardiologist, was developed to normalize blood sugar levels, decrease LDL cholesterol levels (the bad cholesterol), reduce waist–hip ratios, and control food cravings. It recommends plenty of high-fiber foods, lean proteins, and healthy fats, while cutting out breads, rice, pastas, and fruits. Portion sizes are unrestricted.

There are three described phases of the diet. The first is the strictest one and lasts two weeks. In this induction phase, you can expect to lose between eight and thirteen pounds. You eat normal size portions of meat, chicken, turkey, fish, and shellfish as well as plenty of vegetables, eggs, cheese, and nuts. You have olive oil on your salads and also get to have midmorning and midafternoon snacks. The objective is to never feel hungry. You'll even have dessert after dinner, with plenty of coffee, tea, and water. However, these are the foods you won't eat: bread, rice, potatoes, pasta, baked goods, candy, cake, cookies, ice cream, sugar, beer, wine, and alcohol.

In phase 2, where you remain until you've reached your weight loss goal, you start adding things back in, such as healthy carbs: fruit, whole-grain bread, rice, pasta, and sweet potatoes. At this phase, you can expect to lose about one pound a week.

In phase 3, which is supposed to last the rest of your life, it will no longer feel like you're dieting, just eating normal foods in normal size portions. When over-indulging gets out of hand, as it does for most of us once in a while, it's suggested that you go back to phase 1 for a week or two.

The South Beach diet, which appeals with six daily eating occasions and recipes, means to insure that you never feel hungry. In fact, feeling hungry, which prompts cravings, must be avoided. If you do experience hunger, you are being too stingy with your portion sizes. The author promises that you will lose belly fat first and the rest of your excess fat after that. Exercise is not mentioned. Although it isn't totally consistent with the "Ten Rules for Healthy Eating," it comes closer than other popular diet plans. All three diets help you to take weight off, and all three anticipate that you'll be on a diet for the rest of your life. That means you always will be struggling with temptation. If you backtrack, you start all over with the strictest level again.

The plan that I think works best for most of us is one that is not a diet in the usual sense, it's a way of eating that feels normal. You don't have to wrestle with temptations because nothing is forbidden. You're advised to eliminate bad fats, sugars, starches, and supersized portions. As long as you get your full complement of essential portions, the theory goes, you'll have little room or desire for treats and comfort foods. All the evidence is not in yet, but in six months, people who have tried this approach, which doesn't require counting calories, grams, or points, seem to like it. They lose weight effortlessly and lower their blood cholesterol and triglyceride levels, as well as their blood pressure.

Life in the Restricted Lane

Scientists at the Monell Chemical Senses Center in Philadelphia have been studying how food and beverage choices are guided by a combination of taste, smell, and chemosensory irritation, what we know as flavor. In one set of studies, researchers examined the eating behaviors of rats to look for the triggers that prompt binge behavior in yo-yo dieters. Scientists discovered that just a taste of a high-sugar, high-fat "forbidden food" eaten close to the time of a stressful experience acted as a "primer," compelling the rats to binge on any available food, not just the primer food. In dieting terms, these studies suggest that if you give in to a crumb of temptation at the wrong time, like when you're experiencing high stress, you may be doomed to keep on binging even when the stress is gone. So far the study has only been tried on rats. But if it bears out in people, as the researchers expect it will, weight loss will no longer be considered a simple, "calories in, calories out" issue.

The Monell study illustrates just one aspect of the chemical communications between your mouth, mind, and body that drive you to overindulge despite your best intentions. But there is a ray of hope in this gloomy picture. If you don't experience stress within twenty-four hours of giving in to temptation, you probably won't feel the need to binge.

Monell's researchers are also exploring how chemicals that affect smell and taste can influence the desire for, as well as the digestion and metabolism of food. Early studies indicate that the more intense the smell and taste of a food, the less you will eat of it, and conversely, the more bland a food is, the more you're likely to eat.

Our Paleolithic ancestors didn't have the problem of dealing with excessive amounts of attractive food in the environment. They didn't drive to work each morning past doughnut shops where you could buy a Diet Coke and a hot doughnut that melts in your mouth. Nutritionally, neither the Coke nor the doughnut has any redeeming qualities. Doughnuts are loaded with refined sugar and white flour that lard on the trans-fats (bad fats) that increase heart disease. Diet Coke contains caffeine, glutamate, and aspartame, all of which are addictive. Worse, your gut "reads" the artificial sweetness of the Diet Coke as if it was real sugar and orders the release of enough insulin from your pancreas to clear out the excess sugar from your bloodstream. The more frequently insulin is pumped out in this way, the more your tissues are likely to develop resistance to it, and the more insulin you'll need. Repeated often enough, this scenario can lead to type 2 diabetes.

One doughnut is not going to kill you, but it could trigger binging behavior, not only eating more doughnuts, but also everything in your pantry, fridge, or freezer. Dr. Kathleen Keller, an appetite researcher at the St. Luke's-Roosevelt Hospital Obesity Research Center in New York City, says food companies conduct extensive research to find the ideal sugar/fat proportions that are the most enticing and irresistible. Overweight and obese individuals experience a double whammy from these attempts to coerce us into taking another bite of the (candy) apple.

Brain scans using MRI (magnetic resonance imaging) technology demonstrate that lean and obese people react differently to the taste of high-fat, high-sugar foods as well as to the sight of them. Many obese people need only to look at or smell high-sugar, high-fat foods to crave them. Items like doughnuts, full of refined white flour and fat, raise our level of serotonin, the good mood hormone, and dopamine, the hormone responsible for pleasurable sensations. That's why, when you're feeling low, these foods reach out to you. Unfortunately, just a taste can sink your weight loss efforts by prompting binge behavior. What you can do is avoid temptation. Don't look, don't smell, and don't taste what is irresistible to you.

It's not just about the calories. Intricate and elaborate hormone-brain networks in your body, influenced by the amount of sugar and fat you eat, your sensitivity to the smell and taste of food, and your prior dieting history, influence your ability to shed excess weight. One chemical messenger, leptin, is responsible for controlling both your appetite and how much fat you store around your middle. It does so by taking note of the food energy available in your jelly-belly and the excess sugar in your bloodstream. You may want to get rid of your belly fat, but your brain and liver cells are marching to a different drummer—that of the neurotransmitter leptin.

Leptin's primary objective is to save you from starvation, which your Paleolithic body was designed to withstand. Never mind the adage, "You can never be too thin or too rich." Your brain wants to protect you from dangers such as getting stuck on an ice floe sailing down a swollen river with nothing to eat but your toenails. To your brain, the name of the game is survival, not haute cuisine.

Even though we live in an environment glutted with food and persuasive messages urging us to eat more, our basic nature hasn't changed from the time our ancestors hunted woolly mammoths with spears made of bone and stone. Given our body's propensity to save fat for a rainy day and our jaded taste buds that always want greater food variety and bigger portions, is it any wonder we have so much trouble keeping our calories in line? The first thing to do about this is to protect yourself from food-glutted environments where the right choices can be subverted and from images and messages about your favorite food outlets and eating adventures that await you in fast-food paradises.

Emotional Eating

When brain chemicals drive you to overeat, it is an attempt to shield yourself from painful feelings, says psychotherapist John Ruskan, author of *Emotional Clearing: A Groundbreaking East/West Guide to Releasing Negative Feelings and Awakening Unconditional Happiness*. Overeating suppresses painful feelings we don't want to think about and allows us to delude ourselves into thinking we've gotten rid of the problem. But hurtful or sad feelings keep popping back into our consciousness, and when they do, we may be tempted to drown them out by overeating again.

Ruskan believes that what we're really trying to do is regain control over our lives. But trying to control compulsive eating through willpower alone, instead of confronting and coming to terms with the feelings that caused the overeating, is an impossible task. On an emotional level, eating is identified with being cared for, nourished, and mothered, and with mothering others. Our inability to feel satisfied can reflect experiences with a mother who was emotionally unavailable, unaffectionate, or who did not validate our feelings. Pain from these experiences can give rise to compulsive overeating as well as other addictive behaviors (alcohol, tobacco, drugs). Unless released, these painful memories can continue to sabotage you even after you succeed in reaching your weight goals.

Jodi's Story

Jodi Edwards was forty-seven, the bright, successful manager of a school for disabled children. When a new women's gym came to town, she joined and went on the weight loss diet the gym recommended. She weighed 287 pounds when she started working out five times a week and eating according to the plan.

Jodi lost one hundred pounds in the course of a year and won an award for the most weight lost by any club member. She looked fantastic! Even her neighbors didn't recognize her. Jodi was proud of her weight loss and basked in how everyone said she looked gorgeous and sang praises for her accomplishment. But shortly after her one-year anniversary as a club member, she reported that she was finding it hard to stay motivated and focused on losing more weight. She was working out twice and sometimes three times a week instead of five, and when she came to work out she would talk about the marvelous dinners she and her husband were enjoying every weekend. Now that she was svelte, he was wining and dining her. The old Jodi never wanted to talk about anything that wasn't "legal" on the diet. The new Jodi did, and her weight was slipping. When we talked about it, she blew it off. "I just need to get my concentration back and I've been too busy to do it," she told me, "I made a bargain with myself—I'll eat what I want now, but not when I'm back on the diet."

You're in trouble when you promise yourself good behavior later in exchange for bad behavior now. And who was Jodi making a bargain with? Herself. The longer you put off changing your eating habits, the longer it will take to clean up the mess. But what can you do when the desire for unrestricted food is so strong that you repeatedly sabotage yourself?

For many of us, eating is a way to relax, calm down, and chase away the blues. When you're gripped by an urge to overeat, instead of diving into the cookie box, breathe! Breathe in, and breathe out. Sit quietly and picture yourself calmly telling a friend about the feelings that are driving you to binge. As you become aware of those feelings, the compulsion to eat "forbidden foods" will release its hold on you. Your emotional equilibrium will be a sign that you no longer need to bury your uncomfortable feelings beneath a wall of food. We need our feelings. We need to feel them. That's what makes us human.

A Natural Way to Control Appetite

According to Dr. Alan Hirsch, a psychiatrist and neurologist who directs the Chicago-based Smell and Taste Treatment Research Foundation, what we don't realize is that the only way to slim down, avoid rebound, break away from toxic eating patterns, and live a nutritionally balanced life is by harnessing the power of our noses. That's right, our noses! The author of numerous books and over two hundred articles on smell and taste, Dr. Hirsch believes that by enhancing the taste and smell of food you can fool the brain into thinking you've eaten more than you really have, making you feel full faster. But smell and taste can also be used to manipulate you into eating more.

Eric Schlosser, author of *Fast Food Nation*, famously described the manipulation of flavor in most processed foods, citing as one example fast-food french fries whose meaty flavor (from beef tallow added to the cooking oil) makes you want to eat more and more. In addition to beef tallow, other natural fat flavors are used to enhance the taste of processed meats and to replace animal fat in reduced-fat products.

The addition of chicken- and bacon-fat flavors contribute the slippery mouth feel of fat and meat to low-fat burgers and baked chicken nuggets. Corn and potato chips that are baked instead of fried are sprayed with these fats to retain or heighten their flavors. Natural lard, fried, french-fried, fried noodle, fried potato, and fried beef flavors are added to foods after processing as finished flavors. They make us want to eat more, demonstrating that fooling the brain's taste perceptions works two ways. In fact, an entire global chemical flavor industry, headquartered in New Jersey, has grown up around the need for flavors by the processed food industry. Once you've cleared from your palate the strong salty, meaty, sweet, and spicy synthetic tastes that permeate processed, commercial foods, you are able to taste the more subtle flavors of natural foods. People say that they never realized how good fresh organic fruits and vegetables taste, how rich the flavors!

Dr. Hirsch has discovered in the course of his twenty years of research into smell and taste, independent of the food industry, that a special mechanism in your brain is stimulated when you taste specific flavors. The brain equates the amount of food you've eaten with the amount of taste you perceive. Because the sense of taste is 90 percent tied to the sense of smell, Dr. Hirsch developed taste/smell crystals that, when sprinkled on food, naturally stimulate chemosensory receptors, causing you to eat less than you would normally. In a study of ninety-two overweight individuals who used the crystals on every food they ate for six months, the average weight loss was thirty-four pounds.

Based on his extensive research, Dr. Hirsch has developed a proprietary flavor product called Sprinkles that is now on the market. The Sprinkles are added to every portion of food you eat, sweet ones for sweet foods, and salty ones for savory foods. The intensified flavor experienced with Sprinkles cuts your appetite and most people eat about 50 percent less than they do without the flavor enhancers. For more information about Sprinkles, Dr. Hirsch, or the Smell and Taste Research Foundation, visit his website at www.scienceofsmell.com.

More Evidence to Support a Plant-Based Diet

The largest and most important study of diet and disease ever conducted, the China Study, led by distinguished nutrition scientist Dr. T. Colin Campbell of Cornell University, charts the path to wellness and fitness among rural Chinese who eat mainly plant-based diets with relatively little animal protein. According to Dr. Campbell, "In

China, we found people whose diets ranged from being very low in fat (6 percent of calories) and almost entirely made up of foods of plant origin, to diets that contained significant amounts of animal products and even higher amounts of fat (24 percent of calories). Dietary protein levels also vary across China.

"We compared people on diets that are virtually nil in animal protein with those for whom animal protein is upwards of 20 to 30 percent of total protein intake, contrasted with levels of 60 to 80 percent in many Western diets, and Chinese cholesterol levels that go, on average, from about 90 mg per 100 ml to about 170, contrasted with typical North American levels that range between 180 and 260. The cholesterol levels we see in North America are associated with the emergence of various cancers, diabetes, and heart disease that increasingly plague the world's developed nations."

The situation in rural China, says Dr. Campbell, is like that of the West before the industrial revolution, when cancers and cardiovascular diseases were much less prevalent. Dr. Campbell believes that in order for there to be a significant change in the disease picture in North America, a substantial change in American dietary patterns must occur, from animal-based to plant-based diets. He acknowledges that although the biology of diet and disease relationships is complex and easily misunderstood, the main nutritional conclusion from the China study is that the greater the consumption of a variety of good-quality plant-based foods, the lower the risk of Western diseases, and 80 to 90 percent of the cases of cancers, heart problems, diabetes, hypertension, and other life-threatening disorders in the West could be prevented.

For all of us who have downed protein like a lifeline in our titanic battles with bulges, this may sound like the final nail in our coffins. Protein helps us quell our cravings, energizes us before and after our fitness workouts, and promises to kick our bodies into "turbo-charged" fat burning by creating more muscle and less fat in our bodies. A low-protein prescription may save our lives, but without the ability to whittle down our waistlines, will life be worth living?

If you need more background on the food quality over quantity argument, a 2005 study by Stanford University researchers, reported in the *Annals of Internal Medicine*, compared the effects of a typical low-fat diet, recommended by the American Heart Association and others, with one including a lot more vegetables, beans, and whole grains (plant-based foods). In just four weeks, the people eating the plant-based diet had more than twice the drop in cholesterol levels as those following a conventional low-fat diet. The leader of the study, assistant professor of medicine Christopher Gardner, says that doctors have always emphasized what to avoid. This study shows that they ought to be telling their patients what to eat: more fresh, plant-based foods, less protein-rich foods, never mind the fat levels.

Secrets of Success

Most people stop dieting before reaching their weight loss goal (97 percent of us) and eventually regain what they lost. You may tell yourself that you ditched your diet because it's no longer working (you've stopped losing weight), but the real answer is that you became bored with dieting and tired of the bland sameness of the foods that have stopped tasting good. The excitement wears off when the first surge of weight loss is over and a slower rate of loss begins. That's the time to kick things up a notch by revving up the duration of walks and workout repetitions in the gym. But also make sure that you are not sabotaging yourself by eating too few calories. If you've dropped below 1,200 calories a day, you are turning down your metabolic fires. Just by recalibrating what you're doing, you'll turn up the excitement level as you see new, improved weight loss results.

But whether you prefer the low-carb or low-fat diet lifestyle, or you just enjoy counting calories, the problem may be not in the program but in the fact that you are trying to follow an exacting eating plan. What if, instead of a program, you just started to follow the recommendations in the "Ten Rules for Healthy Eating" and the food Guide for Healthy Eating in this book? Don't think of what you're doing as following a diet, because if you do, you will come to a point when you will say, to heck with it! And you'll be right back where you were before you started the plan. Some commercial weight loss programs try to handle this problem before it overcomes their members.

WeightWatchers does it by making you a member for life and signing you up for their maintenance program after you've completed the weight loss phase. The message here is that you'll always be on a diet, no matter what dress or pants size you've achieved, to keep the lost weight off. Curves, on the other hand, tells you they can help you recalibrate your eating and your damaged metabolism so you never need to diet again once you've reached your goal weight. They provide you with tools to get back on track quickly if the problem of weight gain starts to get out of control. Both programs claim great success, although statistics are not available. What you can do is to follow a plan or the ten rules for at least six weeks. Measure your progress; assess whether you think you can do it for another six weeks; and up the ante slightly on your activity and exercise levels. Make sure you're not leaving out any vital foods or nutrients. If you're feeling good, stay with the program for another six weeks. Research shows that people who keep trying eventually will be successful. So set goals, build in rewards, do it with a buddy, go to classes or dieting parties and recipe swaps, and use every trick you can to make this voyage fun and fresh.

Yet, most people say they can't lose weight, no matter how hard they try. Which really means they've tried most of the popular diet plans and have failed to achieve their weight loss goals. They are convinced that they failed, not the program, and that they are not cut out for losing weight. And that's the problem. As long as they see the road to weight loss as "over there," separate and apart from the road to real food and eating, which is "over here," they are like the horse that's been coerced to leave the barn to go through his paces and is heading back to the barn from the moment he leaves it. Instead, see weight loss as a process, a series of small changes and adaptations that will move you closer to where you want to be. Don't listen to the inner voice that says you can't, you won't, you haven't . . . you have three things on your side: foods you really enjoy, friends you enjoy sharing with, and a way to relieve frustration, recognizing that as long as you're losing or making the moves to lose, you're a success! It's not all about numbers on the scale; it's about the power of your convictions.

But before you begin your journey of healthy weight loss, make sure that your health and hormones are in good working order and not slowing you down. If they are, you're going to need medical backup.

I'm reminded of a friend who is a classic "foodie" with significant weight to lose who expressed a desire for my help in losing. I started to help him only to discover that he had a million reasons why what I suggested wasn't going to work. In the end, my friend was afraid of losing part of his personal and cultural identity as a bon vivant, a man of cultivated tastes in wine, food, and women. My friend, whom I shall call Charlie, was heading home to the comfort and security of the barn from the moment he started down the road to weight loss.

Charlie could have adapted a plan that would have allowed him his role as a food and wine savant while presenting dinners for his friends that were only slightly "lightened." By following a controlled eating plan most days of the week, he would have room for wine and somewhat richer fare one day a week. Exercise, starting with walking daily and eating by the clock to make sure he isn't ravenous between meals would make it easier for him to stay on the program. From a health point of view, Charlie needed a cholesterol and triglyceride-lowering diet with fewer packaged and convenience foods. That means planning his meals and snacks in advance and believing that he can lose weight. He says he plans to follow the eating plan in this book when it comes out.

Healthy eating at any weight appears to be a tall order in North America. Only about three in one hundred people, twice as many women as men, are able to maintain their ideal weight, eat the recommended minimum of five daily servings of fruits and vegetables, and exercise for at least thirty minutes three times a week, the brace of lifestyle behaviors consistent with long-term good health. Eating well and feeling good can lead to making other positive changes in your health behaviors, a lifestyle approach that emphasizes eating a variety of wholesome foods and maintaining regular physical activity. It's the best and cheapest health insurance you can buy.

The choice is yours. In this chapter, you've encountered the latest thinking about diet and weight loss and several simple, easy, and delicious plans to follow if you decide to take up the challenge. There's no one perfect diet that works for everyone, but in this chapter I have described several that have worked for millions of dieters, at least for a while. You won't feel hungry following these plans, and you probably won't have the urge to binge. So take heart and take action. It will not only help you to look and feel better, but it also may save your life.

To conclude this guide, in Chapter 10, we discuss some of the ways you can participate in protecting your community's food at the local level. You and your children deserve the safest and most healthful food and water you can have. Don't rely on big government or big business to do it for you without your input. You'll find ideas for becoming part of the solution and ways you and your neighbors can take meaningful action in your hometown and community to make food and water safer.

Food for Change

We need activism that is not one of reaction but of initiation, one in which people of good will everywhere set the agenda . . . that doesn't just respond to the evils of the present but calls forth the possibilities of the future.
We need a revolution of hope.

—Rebecca Solnit

Before writing this chapter, I participated in a health fair at one of the local public elementary schools in my hometown. Sixty children in grades one through four were escorted by their teachers into classrooms in which two dozen community "experts"—from the local ambulance rescue team to a yoga instructor and myself—shared what we thought was important for children to know. But what was striking was what the children already knew.

In my room, we sampled 100 percent whole-grain sourdough bread and freshly cut raw veggies while talking about the five colors of nutrition and everyday foods versus once-in-a-while foods. I was amazed by two things. First, although the children had just finished lunch, they ate the whole-grain bread and veggies enthusiastically, even asking for seconds as they left the room to go to their next station. Second, they knew a lot about where the foods we sampled came from—from the ground, not a store, they told me, and when I asked what was good and bad to eat, they responded, fruits and veggies are good and sugary sodas and doughnuts are bad. What they know may not equate with what they like to eat, but what they don't know doesn't stand a chance of affecting their food choices now or later. What they know is important to their future.

A few kids in each group said that what was sprayed on plants to kill weeds and bugs was bad, and that it was better not to spray. Another said he liked to help his father cook supper. Several others mentioned eating bean curd (tofu). Now please understand, our community is a small, low-wage village within a rural agrarian county, not a Brie-and-Bordeaux suburb of a major metropolitan area. Although there is great concern for the health and nutritional status of this generation of American children, these children were learning, tasting, and thinking about things that I never considered at their age. There's hope, I told myself. This is the generation that can bring about a great health and nutrition transformation in the country.

I want to believe that, but it's easy to become cynical when available research is ignored rather than applied to reduce skyrocketing rates of diet-related diseases. A lack of faith in science that runs counter to leadership's opinions and self-interest lock us in surreal, repetitive battles already won on scientific fields of combat. Science has always been considered subversive by those who fear the free flow of ideas as undermining to their interests. This is the reason nutrition research is only seen as valuable when it bolsters rather than challenges commercial interests.

Benefits of Nutrition Research

One thing I learned working in the government was that there are no gratuitous acts. Actions and reactions are designed to control the agenda, limit public access to potentially damaging information, and protect under-the-radar arrangements between commercial interests and government agents. Those who work for the government put up with this coziness so that the work of the people can go on, never imagining that these relationships are only the beginning—not the end—of the unraveling of public protections.

The pressure for rapid development of new technologies that have the potential to reinvent our world drives many policymakers even when these developments have the potential to harm the public. Take the example of toxic ingredients in foods. Genetic damage from toxic products can be passed on from one generation to the next, so caution must be called for. In Europe they call this the "precautionary principle," and it is applied to all regulations covering food and the environment.

The United States was once the unchallenged leader in nutrition and the environmental safeguards. That is no longer true. We are now battling the stricter standards of European countries that believe it is better to be safe than sorry. Guided by that philosophy, Europeans are requiring chemical companies to present scientific data on the safety of the thirty thousand food chemicals in common use in order to approve them for continued use. The cost of complying with this European directive is estimated at about $7 billion. It is assumed that many chemicals will be found to be unsafe and fall by the wayside, and some companies may have to transform their entire product line.

Years ago, the United States was a pioneer in regulating toxic substances; now Sweden and other European countries are taking aim not just at dioxin in the water but phthalates in nail polish. Americans think of products like cosmetics and food as safe because they're sold openly on the market, which most people think means they have passed some kind of inspection and testing. But these products are largely unregulated and untested, despite the availability of more sensitive tests and greater knowledge of the pathologies caused by industrial chemicals.

We know that low doses of many chemicals in food build up in the body, contribute to learning problems in children, suppress the immune system, increase the risk of cancer, and change sex hormone levels. We know what happens to wildlife exposed to these chemicals but very little about risks to humans. But here in the United States, restricting a chemical under current federal law requires a very tough burden of proof, especially if it can be shown that economic interests of companies would be harmed by a ban on a chemical.

One recent example of how U.S. food rules are weaker and less attuned to public health than those of European countries follows. New research from France has confirmed that the most commonly used herbicide in the world, Roundup, used to kill unwanted grasses and weeds, is much more toxic than the manufacturer, Monsanto, admits. The French study showed that at levels one hundred times lower than the recommended use in farming, Roundup causes reproductive damages and endocrine disruption. Endocrine disruption is when a synthetic chemical absorbed into the body either mimics or blocks hormones and disrupts the body's normal functions. The FDA Office of Plant and Dairy Foods now says that half of the nonorganic produce they have tested in grocery stores contains traceable residues of various pesticides, including Roundup.

The National Resources Defense Council, an environmental health and safety advocacy group, admits that the majority of the two thousand chemicals that come on the market every year in the United States do not go through even the simplest tests to determine their potential toxicity. Even in the few cases where some tests are carried out, no assessment is made of whether a chemical has endocrine-interfering properties.

The issue of health impacts of food and agriculture has been a sensitive one for the government. It is obvious why toxicity might be a sensitive subject for producer-oriented agriculture, but why should the health benefits of nutrition be an issue? The following little known story about how the USDA, at the request of several major drug companies, suppressed a report that documented the magnitude of health benefits that could be obtained from good nutrition may shed some light on the subject. It illustrates how nutrition has been used to justify the agendas of both food and pharmaceutical (pharma) interests.

The Disappearing Report

In 1971, at the request of Congress, a professional analyst working for the Agricultural Research Service of the USDA, C. Edith Weir, produced a 120-page report on the benefits of human nutrition research for human health. It was a time when it was hard to determine what, if anything, the government was spending on nutrition research, other than on the feeding of farm animals and keeping sick people alive on tube or intravenous feedings, or therapeutic diets.

The Congressional Research Service reported that it could find very few hard dollars earmarked for human nutrition research in government budgets. But Edith Weir, a meticulous researcher, working in a lonely cubbyhole on the agricultural farm in Beltsville, Maryland, where farm-related research was headquartered, had scoured national databases to find statistics on the ten leading causes of death in the United States and the strongest cases that could be made as to which deadly killers were caused by poor or imbalanced nutrition.

Weir's work demonstrated rather dramatically that improper or inadequate nutrition was responsible for seven out of ten of the leading causes of death and disability in the United States, problems that had the potential to be reversed by better nutrition. The report was a bombshell. Congressional hearings on the report inspired Senator

George McGovern and his staff of public health experts to put together the landmark *Dietary Goals for the United States*, the study that pressured the USDA and DHHS (Department of Health and Human Services) to publish the *Dietary Guidelines for Americans*, the first official government publication advising the public to change their eating habits in order to avoid common chronic diseases. The previous dietary advice from the USDA, popularly known as the "Basic Four Food Guide," didn't acknowledge that food had anything to do with chronic disease, hiding behind the old rubric, "We just don't know enough to say anything yet."

Weir's report, scheduled to be printed and distributed through the U.S. Government Printing Office, suddenly disappeared. It never was published, from that time until this. The U.S. Senate later held hearings on the report and pushed the USDA to issue diet and health guidelines for the first time. It wasn't until 1980, more than a decade after Edith Weir's report was suppressed, that the first federal dietary guidelines were issued.

The dietary guidelines published in 1980 were meant to be accompanied by a thirty-page sister publication that offered menus and recipes for easy ways to put the guidelines to work. *Ideas for Better Eating: Menus and Recipes to Make Use of the U. S. Dietary Guidelines*, developed by me and my USDA staff, was never released. Like Edith Weir's extraordinary report, however, after the initial printing and circulation to members of Congress who had requested it, instead of publishing the recipe booklet as planned, the publication was suppressed, never to be seen again. It wasn't the only nutrition publication suppressed at the USDA. In fact, I probably hold the dubious distinction of having had four of them suppressed: "FOOD I" and "FOOD II" (popular nutrition and health magazines), *Ideas*, and the original version of the food pyramid guide. Either I was doing something wrong or somebody didn't want the nutrition message to change and gain new popularity. The publications, which had been extensively reviewed and edited in the run-up to publication, were suppressed because the guidance in them was based on new diet advice.

The first pyramid food guide, originally developed by me and my staff with the guidance of numerous academic experts, was scheduled for release within months of the dietary guidelines publication. Even after the USDA, at the political level, made extraordinary and scientifically unsupported changes to the pyramid, including moving grains from the tip of the pyramid (with sugars and fats) to the base and adding inflated serving recommendations, the pyramid was deemed too risky to agricultural interests to be made public, and despite its up-graining, it too was suppressed. The food pyramid would, eventually, reappear in altered form in 1992, eleven years after it was first scheduled for release, but only after more foot-dragging by the USDA. Marion Nestle, in her book *Food Politics*, details the various shenanigans and stratagems that mired the pyramid in the muddy waters of the Potomac in the 1990s.

The food pyramid guide finally was released as a result of the ruckus kicked up by the USDA's heavy-handed attempts to suppress it. It was the first time the USDA endorsed a healthy eating message that called for eating less of anything; in this case, less sugar, fat, meat, alcohol, and salt/sodium. The message to "eat less" has never been so explicit again, with each successive new edition of the guidelines, which are reissued every five years, crafted with softer, more blurred messages than the previous version. The USDA's latest dietary advice, illustrated on the website mycalories.gov, sounds a nostalgic theme last heard in the era of the basic four food groups: "All food is good food!"

It's easy to be frustrated when the health consequences of eroding food protections are ignored by those responsible in our government. But some critics believe that the government shouldn't be telling people what to eat, and they downplay government responsibility over food, water, and air standards. Yet 97 percent of the deaths and disabilities in this country not caused by war are attributable to poor-quality food, water, and air, and our tax dollars foot the bills.

Let's imagine for a moment what a healthy food environment might look like. One thing we could do is to replace junk food and drinks with healthier foods like fruits, veggies, and whole grains. If these foods were cheaper and more plentiful, more people would buy them, and money raised by "sin taxes" on unhealthy products could be used to subsidize them. That is the opinion of no less a health authority than Dr. Andrew Weil (*Self Healing*, November 2002), based on a proposal advocated by Dr. Kelly Brownell, a leading advocate for changing the food environment that contributes to our obesity crisis.

"Twinkie taxes" on snack foods, candy, and soda have already been introduced in eighteen states. They are being fought tooth and nail by sugar and food industry lobbyists in every state legislature, so it's not certain that they will survive, but at least they are in play. Find out if a "Twinkie tax" has been introduced in your state legislature and make your opinion known.

Local Is the New Global

What we buy, cook, and eat is local. It may come to us from far away, but we don't buy it far away. We have the choice of what food to buy and where to buy it. That is the fragile strand that is our nutrition lifeline in these times. As winds shift toward a global, centralized, and controlled food supply, we can choose to be part of a regional agricultural network that emphasizes locally grown food for local consumption. Such a turnaround will save energy, create jobs, and produce more healthful and enjoyable fresh food for our communities.

"Fresh" is a relative term. "Fresh food" in your supermarket means that produce has traveled a distance of between 1,500 and 2,500 miles to get to you. It takes a week for fresh foods grown on one coast to be sold on the other. Not to mention the costs. Hiring a truck to carry twelve hundred cartons of strawberries from one coast to the other costs between five and six thousand dollars. That's five dollars per unit without even considering the cost of growing the fruit or the fuel to convey it from coast to coast. Grapes and cucumbers imported from Chile or Mexico take one to two weeks to get to your store, including time for USDA inspections. Transporting more local produce in light trucks within your state could save a great deal of money in fuel and labor costs, as well as in reducing vehicle emissions.

Additional savings can come from buying local produce in season. How difficult is it to wait for local strawberries instead of devouring ones shipped in from California or Florida in early spring? Aside from the money you would save on your food bill, buying local pumps money back into the local economy and supports family farms. And it allows you to make a personal connection with growers so what you eat isn't the anonymous product of a faceless company, but the produce of someone whose values you can judge when you meet him or her at the farmer's market. Does he care about the land and his customers? Does he avoid using harmful pesticides and genetically manipulated seeds, and does he treat his animals humanely? Wouldn't you rather buy food from someone who can answer yes to those questions?

In my local farmer's market in Bellows Falls, Vermont, in addition to fresh fruit, vegetables, flowers, and ornamentals, we can buy locally made organic spelt breads, homemade fruit breads and pies, cheeses, pasture-raised beef, lamb, and eggs, maple syrup, jewelry, and crafts. A visit to the market on a Friday afternoon is a social event where you meet friends and neighbors, taste specialties of local chefs, and listen to music. We always have a band and a singer to entertain us. The relaxed, happy atmosphere lends itself to swapping recipes, tasting, sharing gossip, and laughter. It's not just a market but a commons where food connects us viscerally and reflects our values as a community.

The organic food we buy there is better tasting, freshly picked, and lasts a week longer than produce from the supermarket. It's a relief to eat fresh, flavorful food after a long cold winter when you were glad for any fruit and vegetables you could find. It's the time to release the week's tensions and turn off the chatter in your mind in response to a smile and an encouraging neighborly word. But be careful, letting down your defenses can be a subversive act. Once you become part of the culture of the farmer's market, you will become addicted to it.

Myths of the Twinkie Police

I wonder if the old-time, relaxed atmosphere of the farmer's market makes some in government nervous that seditious acts are being plotted there. Can they be mistaking whispers about zucchini recipes for talk of insurrection? Concern about new international rules to codify and restrict sales of supplements, vitamins, and minerals in Europe has been heard at my market lately. We are talking about it because we know that anything designed for global trade will soon be the law of our land, too, as our government races to form a borderless world.

People who shop at my farmer's market don't welcome restrictions on the sale of supplements, herbs, or foods. The FDA has been trying to regain authority over supplements since 1994, when the Congress voted that supplements are foods, not drugs, and as such removed them from FDA control. Now, Codex Alimentarius, the World Trade Organization's enforcement code for foods, supplements, and vitamins, is being handed to drug enforcement authorities in Europe, and it could soon be adopted here. Even though the code is wildly unpopular, the U.S. government, for the sake of global trade, must fall in line or risk heavy fines for trading when not in compliance with international law.

Nutrition advocates who want the freedom to buy supplements are taking on the challenge of protecting them from restriction. But the FDA and the drug companies are not happy about the swelling ranks of aroused nutrition consumers. In response to renewed grassroots activism around international food rules, lobbyists have launched a smear campaign against nutrition advocates!

It's a free country, of course, especially for lobbyists who don't like their golden fleece exposed by health-minded consumer groups and legislators. Rumors started by lobbyists and PR flacks charge that crazed nutrition nannies in tennis shoes are ready to burst into your home and raid your pantry and fridge to confiscate every last Twinkie and Hershey's kiss. The lobbyists worry about clinic nutritionists counseling heart patients to follow a nearly vegetarian diet and schools full of frolicking kids soon to be deprived of vending machines dispensing essential Cokes and Gummy Bears. The lobbyists call the campaign against obesity an "un–American assault" on the freedom to choose (to swallow junk foods and drinks), a right that is surely protected under the First Amendment. It's hard enough to teach your children good food habits without schools (needing money for sports uniforms) succumbing to powerful lobbying interests that want to be the dominant brand in your child's world.

In Connecticut, Governor Jodi Rell vetoed a bill that would have rid Connecticut schools of soda and junk food. Similar scenarios are playing out across the nation where high–paid food lobbyists from multinational corporations are setting up shop in state legislatures, outmaneuvering and outflanking the underfunded efforts of overworked educators and nutritionists with handfuls of cash and political payola.

With rising rates of obesity and diabetes among school-children, the continued sale of junk foods and drinks in the schools goes against common sense, yet venal corporations are willing to place corporate profits ahead of the health of our children. In California, Kentucky, Arizona, and Oregon, legislation to ban junk food from the schools has been defeated by lobbyists' efforts. From this, students learn that what we tell them is not as important as what we sell them. Where the lobbyists have won, children's health is for sale.

Seattle is one bright spot in this otherwise dismal picture. The school board, determined to provide students with healthy food options, has unanimously approved one of the strongest policies in the country, banning the sale of all foods containing high levels of sugar and fat, improving school meals, and outlawing contracts with soft drink vendors for "exclusive pouring rights." The policy also directs school meal directors to offer fresh, local, organic, non–genetically modified, nonirradiated, unprocessed food whenever possible.

Historically, the USDA has made the school lunch program a dumping ground for surplus fatty animal products; excess milk, butter, and cheese; canned vegetables and fruits; white-flour breads; and bakery products. Today, many school meal programs have been hijacked by powerful fast-food interests and the processed food/sugar lobbies that control both the brands of foods and drinks children consume and even the nutrition messages they hear in their schools.

Why should global food corporations worry about the paltry efforts of a few pronutrition voices to make the country healthier? You'll have to ask the ten to twelve corporations who are most militant about silencing the critics. They tolerate no opposition to their single-minded purpose of controlling the world's food supply.

But you can talk back to the junk and fast-food lobbies by voting with your pocketbook and wallet. It's time to punish the bad actors who are waging war against our children, and it's past time to insist on healthy eating habits for our kids in schools and in our communities. As to the freedom to eat french-fried toxic foods containing cancer-causing acrylamide and white-flour bread containing the diabetes-causing ingredient alloxan, tell the junk food moguls: "Not here, not now!"

The government has been spending about $3 million a year on its five-a-day campaign promoting fruit and vegetable consumption, but McDonald's spends $1 billion a year encouraging people to eat hamburgers, fries, and soft drinks. Soda and other sweet drinks are now the main source of calories in American diets, an honor previously held by white bread. That's why doctors and nutritionists want to declare war on the promotion of poor eating and drinking habits that "supersize" such health problems as diabetes, heart disease, and cancer.

In addition to overhauling vending machines and school meals, advocates are talking about increasing no-cost healthy offerings like free fruits and vegetables in cafeterias and instituting a public awareness campaign to get people off their couches and into exercise programs.

It took the antitobacco lobby thirty years to turn back big tobacco. But now, by a combination of city ordinances, tobacco taxes, and massive public information efforts to spread the word about the harmfulness of tobacco, there is a 50 percent reduction in smoking by men and a 25 percent reduction in smoking by women, as well as a trending down of lung cancer rates. How do we know the same approach would work as well for nutrition? An ad that ran in West Virginia for six weeks showing the artery-clogging fat of whole milk resulted in soaring sales of skim milk. We know that advertising works, and we know that when junk food is not in kids' faces, they don't think about it. But a campaign against junk food would face the same stiff opposition from the multibillion-dollar food industry that marked the tobacco wars. It would also be more complicated than just telling people not to smoke. People have to eat, and that means learning about the right foods.

Advocates argue that just a one-cent tax on soda could raise $1.5 billion a year in revenue that could be used to finance health education and fitness programs in communities. How about for every fast-food outlet in your town a fitness center where kids and families can play is created? Or having candy-free aisles in supermarkets where mothers can shop with their kids without battling them over junk food? One big supermarket chain in Britain is planning to use a red, yellow, and green light system on shelves labeling to designate the nutritional quality of the foods on the shelves. Instead of displaying candy and other junk foods at the checkout counters, stores display snacks that are more nutritionally valuable.

If we start thinking about what makes our lives better and healthier, we may find that there is room for everyone to get what they need in our democracy. These are bedrock American values. We have the right to healthier food, not just window dressing to make foods look healthier. And we have the power of the purse and the vote to turn things around.

Consider a penny tax on every food item that contains more than 10 percent of its calories from refined sugars and a dramatic reduction in the number of junk food ads on TV, especially during children's programming. These changes would support parents' efforts as gatekeepers of good nutrition for their children. Too often now, we tie parents' hands and silence their messages. Parents, not cereal boxes, are the most important nutrition educators in the land. Don't buy in to smear campaigns that brand those who advocate for nutrition as the "food police."

If we're serious about improving children's health, we need to celebrate the pleasures of healthy eating in every way we can. But don't underestimate the power of the junk food companies who will try to seduce us in every way they can.

An Agenda for Change

What will it take to honestly confront the problems of cheaply produced, toxic ingredients in food, a compromised water supply, and widespread nutritionally impaired health? Never mind how we got to this point. We need to take stock honestly, without making war against those who are carrying the message.

We need to talk to our leaders, politicians, financiers, and corporate executives and tell them that their "bigness" is not a free pass to promote greed, indifference, damage, and control without regard for the public good or the environment. We shouldn't trust leaders from any sphere who profligate our country's wealth and resources, wrecking the land and our children's future.

We mustn't compromise the health of our children and our communities. We don't have to rely on giant corporations to raise our meat and grow our corn, process our vegetables and market them to us locally if they are not willing to make certain these foods are free from avoidable risks.

Some risks are unacceptable, such as those from bioengineered foods shown to be harmful to animals and from meats contaminated with mad cow disease, which has been covered up by the U.S. government for over a decade. There is no cure for mad cow disease. The incompetent testing program conducted by the USDA, in light of the British experience with this horrific disease just one decade ago, makes one wonder about the sanity of policymakers who can't seem to find the right tests to determine which cows have it and should not be brought to market. Perhaps they are doing us a favor, helping us to decide that the only safe meat to buy is organic and pasture-raised. Maybe this tragicomedy of errors will wake us up, finally.

The Edible City

San Diegans are setting aside tracts of land inside the city for organic farming and creating a regional agriculture policy that emphasizes locally grown food for local consumption. In San Diego County, 95 percent of the food produced is exported, and 95 percent of what is consumed is imported. The city is waking up to the realization that it just doesn't make sense. The county is making available to residents unused, available municipal land to grow local produce, and San Diegans are seizing the opportunity.

This program is part of a growing national urban agriculture trend. Across the country, community gardeners, backyard gardeners, food banks in vacant lots, parks, greenhouses, roof tops, balconies, window sills, ponds, rivers, and estuaries are a part of a bourgeoning North American urban agriculture initiative. Today, one-third of the two million farms in the United States are within metropolitan areas, and they produce 35 percent of the country's food.

The trend fits well with another one—hospitals offering fresh food, raised locally or organically, in their cafeterias and directly to patients in their rooms. Hospitals are major buyers and providers of food in their cafeterias, patient rooms, and vending machines. The recognition that good food can speed healing has spurred hospitals to start buying organic and local fresh foods to serve their patients and staff.

One of these developments has been instituted at Kaiser Permanente, which has been awarded the health insurance industry's prestigious Ellis J. Bonner Community Leadership Award for its Farmers' Market initiative, helping to create twenty-two farmer's markets operating at different Kaiser facilities around Northern California. There is a plan to expand to twenty-nine by December 2005. Other health-care facilities with ties to farmer's markets include the National Institutes of Health (Maryland), Duke University Medical Center (North Carolina), Bartels Lutheran Nursing Homes (Iowa), Cancer Treatment Centers (Illinois and Oklahoma), and Fletcher Allen Medical Center (Vermont). In San Antonio, five hospital systems are working together to introduce healthier offerings in their vending machines.

For more information and a complete report on this exciting trend, visit the the Institute for Agriculture and Trade Policy (IATP) website at iatp.org/foodandhealth. IATP is a member of Health Care Without Harm, an international coalition of four hundred-thirty organizations in fifty-two countries working to transform health care so it is no longer a source of harm to people and the environment. The IATP Food and Health Program raises awareness about environmental pollutants in food and from food production as well as their demonstrated or possible impacts on human health. IATP educates consumers to make healthier choices about the food they buy and also educates policymakers to make more informed decisions. They also work to provide farmers with markets for healthy, sustainably produced food. IATP recognizes the need to identify and eliminate the sources of the toxins that find their way into our food. This work is a component of their commitment to sustainable food ecosystems.

Wet and Wild

We take water safety for granted in this country. The National Resources Defense Council (NRDC) says we shouldn't. They estimate that about seven million Americans get sick each year from contaminated tap water, which can be lethal. In June 2003, NRDC carried out a nineteen-city study of drinking water quality. The study team found pollution and deteriorating, out-of-date plumbing—some dating from the nineteenth century—delivering drinking water that could be dangerous to the health of some people, especially the elderly, infants, and the immune-impaired. NRDC urged steps to be taken now to avoid tap water becoming even worse in quality. The report gives grades to each municipal water system and outlines a plan for protecting the nation's drinking water supply.

Did you know that you have a right to know about toxins in your water as well as what is being done to protect residents where problems have been found? In rural areas, water supplies can be contaminated with pesticides and animal and industrial wastes. In cities, ancient equipment and faulty filtering systems can suck up organisms and wastes from the soil and harbor pollution in open reservoirs. The latest contaminant almost universally found in United States water supplies is rocket fuel. It's time to wake up and not take water safety for granted.

Another issue deserving our attention is fluoride. We need to reconsider the safety of fluoridated water supplies. We can no longer justify it on the basis of control of dental caries in children. The best way to protect against caries is by topical fluoride applications not drinking water, studies show. And today both children and adults get too much fluoride—from toothpaste, drinks other than water, and foods. There are no good health reasons for fluoridating drinking water and there is evidence that it damages the thyroid gland, causes mental disorders, and

may set women up for osteoporosis. For more information, read reviews on the subject by Dr. Paul Connett at
www.fluoridealert.org/york-critique.htm and Mary Sparrowdancer at www.rense.com/general45/bll.htm.

Resources to fix the problem of decaying and unsafe
municipal drinking water systems are eroding. At the federal level, a one-third cut in budgetary resources has been
proposed for 2006, and water quality advocates, legislators, and federal and local officials are lost in a blame
game. If the safety of common drinking water is not a
political priority in the United States, do we need to start
thinking about importing safe water from countries such
as Canada, where clean water is a priority?

Consider this about the importance of clean water to
our lives, from the NRDC annual report on water and
oceans: "Whether it's the creek that meanders through
town, the lake where we fish and swim, the majestic
ocean beaches that inspire our awe of nature, or simply the
glass of water we drink, clean water is essential to our
well-being."

Change Happens Slowly

Rebecca Solnit, author and peace activist, reminds us that
progressive action for change is rarely direct. You scatter
seeds not knowing where, when, or how they may sprout.
This chapter is written in the hope that each of you reading this book will carry a seed of change to a place where
it can have great impact long after this book is out of
print.

INDEX